THE REAL IRON LADY

Gillian Shephard

THE REAL
IRON LADY

Working with Margaret Thatcher

Biteback Publishing

First published in Great Britain in 2013 by
Biteback Publishing Ltd
Westminster Tower
3 Albert Embankment
London SE1 7SP
Copyright © Gillian Shephard 2013

Extracts from Margaret Thatcher, *The Path to Power* (1995) and *The Downing Street
Years* (1993) reprinted by permission of HarperCollins Publishers Ltd © Lady
Thatcher. Masses more archive material is available at www.margaretthatcher.org,
the website of the Margaret Thatcher Foundation.

ISBN 978-1-84954-401-6

10 9 8 7 6 5 4 3 2

A CIP catalogue record for this book is available from the
British Library.

Set in Baskerville and Edition

Printed and bound in Great Britain by
CPI Group (UK) Ltd, Croydon CR0 4YY

CONTENTS

ACKNOWLEDGEMENTS

The production of this book has been made possible by the willing and generous help from thirty-six former colleagues, friends and observers of Margaret Thatcher. Without exception, they responded with alacrity and enthusiasm to my request for their recollections of what it was like to work with the 'real' Iron Lady. Their accounts, which are shown in italicised text, provide the core of this book and, I hope, its originality. The excellence of their work has made it possible for me to set it into a historical context and to record my own recollections and thoughts. Thanks to them, the book is fuller and more authoritative than I had thought possible.

Lord Howe of Aberavon kindly selected particularly relevant extracts from his book *Conflict of Loyalty* for me to include, and was happy for me to quote from other parts of that book. Sir John Major, in describing Margaret Thatcher as a 'woman of contrasts' in the piece he wrote for this book, provided its theme; he also gave me access to useful passages from his autobiography. Michael Brunson provided a sparkling account of Mrs Thatcher's relationship with the media, and his autobiography, *A Ringside Seat*, gave more illustrations of the media's attitude towards her, which he made available to me. Lord Cormack, a distinguished former editor of *The House* magazine, allowed me to quote extensively from an interview Margaret Thatcher gave to the magazine in December 1990, two weeks after she stood down, and this forms an authoritative part of the epilogue of this book.

Lord Tyler kindly put me in touch with Ian Beesley, who provided a fascinating civil service insight into working with Margaret Thatcher when she was Prime Minister. Ian Beesley dedicates his contribution to the memory of Clive Priestley, who died in January 2012. Ian succeeded Clive Priestley as Head of the Efficiency Unit in 1983 and writes, 'Clive was "Chief of Staff", as he liked to put it, to Derek Rayner, and was highly thought of by Mrs T.' Especially for Chapter 7, 'Elle a les yeux de Stalin et la voix de Marilyn Monroe', Dr Sophie Loussouarn interviewed Hubert Védrine, former adviser to President Mitterand, and later French Foreign Minister. Baroness Gardner of Parkes asked her daughter, Sarah Joiner, if she would provide her recollections of working in Mrs Thatcher's first general election campaign, which she kindly agreed to do.

The editor of the *Eastern Daily Press* generously agreed

to the reproduction, in the prologue of this book, of the whole of an article from that paper, dated 15 January 1974, describing a visit to Norfolk by Margaret Thatcher when she was Education Secretary. I am also indebted to the *Sunday Times* for allowing me to quote from an article by India Knight (20 November 2011). India Knight's frank admission of her change of attitude towards Margaret Thatcher gave me the inspiration for this book, and the way I approached it. Sarah Baxter also provided invaluable assistance in helping me to contact the *Sunday Times*.

Oral reminiscences came from Lady Ralphs; Allan Rogers, formerly MP for the Rhondda; Sir Donald Stringer; and Milburn Talbot. Mrs Patricia Ramsay, although not directly quoted in the book, gave valuable anecdotes from her friendship with both Denis and Margaret Thatcher.

I have had sterling support from Biteback Publishing, particularly from Hollie Teague and also from Sam Carter and Olivia Beattie. Iain Dale also gave encouragement at all times. Lord Hennessy of Nympsfield gave me *carte blanche* to quote from any of his relevant books, read the manuscript and gave invaluable advice. Keith Simpson MP, with his cheerful encouragement, not only kept me going through some of the longueurs of writing, but also provided the vivid account of a special advisers' meeting at No. 10 in 1988. My stepson, Professor Neil Shephard, read the manuscript and suggested some important changes in emphasis.

Heartfelt thanks are due to the staff of the House of

Lords Library, who willingly and rapidly researched details of dates and parliamentary occasions, and also to the staff of the Swaffham Branch of the Norfolk County Library for obtaining and renewing important reference works. My PA, Margaret West, was, as always, a tower of strength.

Jason Pink helped at key technological moments.

Very special thanks are due to my husband, who put up with the year devoted to this book with his customary good cheer.

PROLOGUE

So read the headline in the *Eastern Daily Press* on Tuesday 15 January 1974. There is no by-line, but a box encloses the words, 'A male colleague covering the visit of Mrs Thatcher to Norfolk last week-end was so impressed by her mastery of facts and femininity that he here gives credit in print – where credit is obviously due!'

Margaret Thatcher was combining official and political duties on a visit to Norfolk and Cambridgeshire on Friday 11 and Saturday 12 January 1974. This was the first time I met her. I was at that time a senior education officer working for the Norfolk County Council, and it had been my job to organise the Norfolk part of the visit, which included the official opening of a new first school, and a tour of other schools, a college, an education study centre in the Broads and an adult education centre in the centre of Norwich. Everyone I knew within the educational world was intrigued by the Secretary of State. She was already a controversial figure. Many were far from supportive, but the then Norfolk Chief Education Officer, Sir Lincoln Ralphs, himself an influential figure on the national education scene, admired her ideas and her vigorous approach. The feeling may have been mutual. Even in those days, it would have been unusual for a Secretary of State to spend a day and a half in one education authority.

The tours were complex and involved many miles of travelling in the rural county, but thankfully my careful arrangements, including the timings, worked, and the weather, although freezing as usual in a Norfolk winter, did not complicate matters.

The *Eastern Daily Press* reporter takes up the tale.

It is ten o'clock on Friday morning at Hethersett and Education Minister Mrs Thatcher is formally opening the Woodside First School. She is bright and alert, relaxed and charming, faultlessly groomed and dressed with careful simplicity in a plain, short-sleeved dress with one small ornament on the shoulder.

During the rest of the day she will be visiting three other schools in mid-Norfolk, then driving across to King's Lynn to see the technical college. Finally to a political dinner in Wisbech, Cambridgeshire, before returning to Norwich to stay the night.

Saturday morning finds her, on the dot at 9.30, at Thorpe

Grammar School, on the outskirts of Norwich. Then out to How Hill to see the county's study centre in the heart of the Broads. Finally back into Norwich to Wensum Lodge, the adult education centre.

And throughout that time a close observer would find her taking a real interest in everything she sees, with time for a word with everyone, from tiny kids to prosy local worthies.

'So what?' you might say. 'All that should be in the line of duty for a Minister.'

But before you reach that conclusion, it might be useful to add that on Thursday, the day before she came to Norfolk, Mrs Thatcher had a morning Cabinet meeting in London. The afternoon and evening were spent in the House of Commons, voting in a crucial economy debate. She left the House at 10.30 p.m., drove to Liverpool Street Station – and arrived at Norwich at 1.36 a.m.

In other words, she had about five hours of sleep before her gruelling Friday began. And while this reporter managed to get a snatched five-minute interview with her before she left for London at lunchtime on Saturday, she was still as relaxed and fluent as if she were settled in a comfortable chair in her own drawing room with an hour to spare for a chat.

On arriving back in London, she had a quick dash to the shops to get some provisions in for the weekend. For Margaret Thatcher still runs her own London home with only a daily help coming in a few mornings a week.

'Just how do you do it?' we asked. 'It is a matter of having the right constitution,' she said in a matter-of-fact way which indicated that she herself didn't see anything particularly special in her demanding routine. 'Happily, I happen to have that constitution,' she adds with a grin.

And the family? 'We always have breakfast together, no matter what. And no matter how late it is when I'm in London, I see my husband and family at the end of the day. I always see there is plenty of food in the fridge. So when I'm not around it is no hardship for them to help themselves.'

Margaret Thatcher spent her two brief nights during the tour with Sir Lincoln and Lady Ralphs at their home in Norwich. Lady Ralphs recalls Mrs T. discussing which dress she should wear for the school opening and visits – she had brought several with her. Finally a red one was chosen, as 'children like red'. As one who also spent a fair amount on the road as Secretary of State for Education, I am deeply impressed by the fact that she not only found time to pack a choice of clothes, but also to discuss which outfit would be most suited to a school visit. She also went out of her way to chat to Lady Ralphs's elderly mother, who was keen to meet the famous guest staying in the house.

My own memories of the occasion are somewhat blurred by my anxiety that everything should go smoothly. An additional complication at the time was that we were in the period of the three-day week, with electricity cuts occurring at any moment.

Photographs reveal her looking relaxed and professional, and me looking somewhat fraught, and unsuitably dressed for a cold January day, in what appears to be an unfashionable spring ensemble. Mrs Thatcher's appearance, on the other hand, won praise from the *Eastern Daily Press* reporter. The caption accompanying her photograph in the article read, 'Mrs Thatcher ideally dressed for Norfolk with a warm, fur-trimmed top coat and simple, elegant day dress to take her through numerous appointments.'

All the qualities of Margaret Thatcher, which, together with her flaws, are the subject of this book, were on show and perceived by the anonymous *Eastern Daily Press* reporter that January in 1974: her professionalism, attention to detail, immaculate appearance, regard for parliamentary conventions and, seemingly, an indefatigable constitution. She would go far, we all thought.

Just over a year later, on 11 February 1975, she did. She became Leader of the Conservative Party, and Britain's first woman Prime Minister in waiting.

It was another twelve years before I went into national politics. My life changed completely in 1975: I married, acquired two stepsons aged ten and fourteen, gave up my professional career and started another in local government. I was impelled to become an MP more out of curiosity about the exercise of power and a desire to change things than because I had been inspired by my encounter with Margaret Thatcher, that January in 1974. Even so, her astonishing rise to become Britain's first woman

Prime Minister and the extraordinary mix of brute force and glamour that she brought to the role were intriguing, as was her ability to run a government and, at the same time, to identify with the concerns of men and women in the street.

Even now, I wonder if the extent of her achievement in becoming Britain's first woman Prime Minister is fully appreciated. When she first entered the House of Commons in October 1959 as the newly elected member for Finchley there were just twelve women Conservative MPs. The odds against her, or any of the other women members, achieving high office, let alone becoming Prime Minister, were overwhelming. Even by 1987, when I entered the Commons and when Margaret Thatcher was nearing the end of her period in office, while 609 men were returned in that election, only an astonishingly tiny number of women – 139 in all – were returned during the whole of the seventy years since women had sat in the House.

There was a similar incredible imbalance in women's representation in the professions and on company boards, examined by a Commission set up by the Hansard Society and published in a report entitled 'Women at the Top' in 1989. There were, for example, only two women Permanent Secretaries within the civil service, no women Law Lords at all and one out of a total of eighty-one High Court Judges. Only 3 per cent of university professors were women and at Oxford only 14 per cent of fellows were women; Cambridge did even worse with a mere 8 per cent. Until 1988, there had never been a woman on the BBC Senior Management Committee. The picture was no better in the business world: of the companies taking part in the Hansard survey, 81 per cent had no woman at all on their main board. And even on the Trades Union Congress, only fifteen seats out of a possible fifty-three were held by women.

This was the context in which Margaret Thatcher became Prime Minister.

As is usual in political life, chance and mishap played quite a substantial role in the course of events which led to her being elected Leader of the Conservative Party. And once she was elected, there were profound misgivings within the party at all levels about whether she, a woman, could actually do the job. There was an enormous amount of prejudice against her, private sneers from some colleagues and from the overwhelmingly male Establishment in Britain.

All Prime Ministers attract harsh and constant criticism. It is part of the job. Margaret Thatcher's critics included those who, legitimately, opposed her policies and her politics – and her sometimes overbearing manner. But one is forced to conclude that others criticised her because of her gender. These critics included some of her close male colleagues whose experience of women was limited to wives, sisters, daughters and secretaries, and who simply had no professional experience of working with women as equals and certainly not as their superiors. Some of the accounts in this book make it clear that their response was to mock and brief behind her back. Legends and myths about Margaret Thatcher endure, but it is perhaps salutary for critics and admirers alike to reflect on the sheer scale of her achievement in becoming Prime Minister in the Britain of the 1970s and 80s.

I was in the House of Commons for only the last two years of Margaret Thatcher's premiership. I can make no claim to have known her, except from afar, or to have been especially favoured by her despite having been appointed by her to my first extremely junior post. However, even from that lowly position, it was possible to perceive that she was able to combine a ferocious appetite for work and the all-important detail of how policies would actually work, with an iron grasp of strategy and long-term aims. I would not claim that this combination of abilities could only be found in a woman leader; on the other hand, no male boss I had, either before or subsequently, had it.

When preparing this book, I decided therefore to ask the contributors if they would concentrate in their accounts on Margaret Thatcher's work habits and her attention to detail, and add any experiences they might have had of her personal kindness or indeed the reverse. I have been overwhelmed by the richness of what they have written and humbled by the care they have taken to give a faithful picture of a woman with whom all of them, without exception, worked more closely than I had the opportunity to do so.

From their accounts, in addition to descriptions of Margaret Thatcher's working practices and countless anecdotes of her personal kindnesses and public furies, other themes have emerged. Her courage is demonstrated over and over again, not just, outstandingly, in the Brighton bomb outrage, but in the Falklands War, where she knew that failure would mean the absolute end of her political career and reputation; in the Miners' Strike and in her confrontations with the trade unions. In today's cynical world, it is touching, however inappropriate that word may seem when applied to Margaret Thatcher, to realise that to the end of her career she retained her belief in and passion for the political process. She combined an intense and unashamed femininity with an ability to cut to the essential issues and make the hard choices; she saw no conflict in that combination. I have particularly enjoyed discovering her pleasure in being an outsider, one who triumphed in spite of, and not because of, her background; and learning more about her international impact, which exists still. Her loyalty and devotion to Denis, her family and close friends and colleagues, and her inimical hostility to those she considered her enemies illustrate someone whom Sir John Major describes, so aptly, as a 'woman of contrasts indeed'.

ONE

'IDLENESS WAS A SIN.'

Margaret Thatcher was never in doubt about what was important in life. She wrote, in *The Path to Power*, 'In my family we were never idle, partly because idleness was a sin, partly because there was so much work to be done, and partly no doubt we were just that sort of people.' That they were indeed 'that sort of people' was corroborated by her friend and contemporary, Margaret Wickstead, quoted by Hugo Young in *One of Us*: 'They were all very serious minded, and they worked too hard. Life was a serious matter to be lived conscientiously.' To Alderman Roberts and his family, time was something to be filled with productive activity: that is, work. Margaret Thatcher told Kenneth Harris that her upbringing had taught her that 'the greatest sin of all was wasting time. Every minute of the day was to be filled with useful occupation. Idleness was a waste... It was very important to use your life to some purpose.'

Many things differentiate Margaret Thatcher from other Prime Ministers, but there is no doubt that among them is this earnest attitude to work. Not for her, in any respect, the cult of the gifted amateur, affected by many other Prime Ministers and perfected by Harold Macmillan. Sir Percy Cradock, foreign affairs adviser to Mrs Thatcher from 1984 to 1992, in his book, *In Pursuit of British Interests: Reflections on Foreign Policy under Margaret Thatcher and John Major*, describes her as

> intensely serious. The camaraderie, the relaxed, jokey, allusive style, the affectation of doing things well without trying, the view of politics and most other things as a game, these expressions of the ruling male culture which with Harold Macmillan had been carried to extreme lengths, all these were alien to her.

The contributors to this book were asked to recall Mrs Thatcher's way of working. Obviously, other strong themes emerged from their accounts, which will be covered in later chapters. But her prodigious energy, her insatiable appetite for facts, her understanding that in politics, possession of the facts is a power in itself, her desire for and attention to detail, her astonishing memory, her expectations of others – alas sometimes disappointed – and, above all, her sheer relish for work all reflect that early upbringing in the household of Alderman Roberts of Grantham. Those who have criticised Margaret Thatcher for having no cultural hinterland, comparing her unfavourably with Denis Healey, for example, simply miss the point. She loved work and, for her, work *was* the hinterland. After she had stood down as Prime Minister, she wrote revealingly in *The Downing Street Years*: 'Throughout my deliberately busy life I have been able to find solace for personal disappointments by forgetting the past and taking up some new venture. Work was my secret elixir.'

When she was asked on the tenth anniversary of her period as Prime Minister if it was not time for her to stand down, she fixed the interviewer, Sir Robin Day, with her intense blue gaze and said, sweetly, 'I see no reason why I should. I enjoy the work.' She meant exactly that.

The accounts which follow include contributions from a No. 10 adviser, a Conservative Party official, a Cabinet minister and a Chief Whip. They describe at first hand the challenges of working with, or perhaps keeping up with, a super-charged Prime Minister who was apparently indefatigable but who also 'always had to be the best briefed'.

Hartley Booth was able to observe Margaret Thatcher at close quarters in two of her roles: as Prime Minister and as constituency MP for Finchley. He was one of seven special advisers working for her at No. 10. He was appointed in 1984 and in 1991 was selected as Conservative candidate for Finchley as successor to Margaret Thatcher when she stood down as an MP.

He recalls working in No. 10 in 1984, when he joined what he describes as a 'lean' Policy Unit.

Margaret's policy was not to surround herself with a huge number of hangers-on and special advisers for paper clips. All of us had to have real practical jobs. My three departments (Home Office, Environment and Lord Chancellor's Department) provided a challenging bundle of issues.

It is a well-known fact that Prime Minister Thatcher was a hard worker. There were lots of examples of her prodigious powers of work. She would call for red boxes even on holidays, was prepared to wade through a pile of red boxes after lengthy foreign trips when anyone else would be wilting, while at the same time insisting that other people have holidays and rest. That last point did not, however, extend to speech writers. The immediacy and importance of producing the right words meant that her speech writing team were not given much rest.

David Willetts and I were in her study one night. Time went on. I believe it was the Spring Party Conference speech in 1987. We looked at our watches. It was one o'clock in the morning. 'Is it one o'clock?' asked Margaret. We were so tired that David and I did not have the spark to say, 'Yes, could we go home now, Prime Minister?' Instead, she said brightly, 'I get a new lease of life at this time of the morning.' And we duly went on until two o'clock, when she drew stumps.

Later that morning in the Cabinet Room, Margaret referred to an item on Farming Today *that she had heard on the radio earlier. The programme came on air at 6 a.m., so she certainly did not have more than four hours' sleep that night.*

Her hard work was effective, but for those around her, it led to her learning things that other Prime Ministers never learned, and caused me ceaseless amazement. As policy adviser for the Home Office, I had to cover prisons and the police. I took the view that prisons were not for prime ministerial intervention, but that police matters would rightly be of interest. So in addition to briefing her on the police, I would regularly flag up just a few paragraphs I thought relevant in Police magazine *for her to read, only to find that she would then read the whole magazine from cover to cover.*

Harvey Thomas, Head of Press, Communication and Presentation at Conservative Central Office for thirteen years from the late 1970s onwards, remembers Margaret Thatcher's ability to dismiss fatigue, apparently at will:

One Saturday during the 1983 election campaign, in the Ballards Lane constituency office in Finchley, Roger Boaden (a senior CCO agent) and myself, a delightful Garden Room girl (a secretary from No. 10) and Mrs T. flopped around a trestle table for a sandwich lunch. It was late-ish in the campaign, and she had afternoon engagements and we were all shattered. I said wistfully and with a mild attempt at humour, 'Well, we've all earned it, and I think it's time for a siesta!' Roger Boaden and our colleague smiled and both said enthusiastically, 'Yes, that's what we need.' I looked across the table at Mrs T. and said, 'Well, that's three of us in favour of a siesta, that's almost unanimous.' With a perfectly straight face she said, 'It's not unanimous, it's a majority of one against.' We all laughed. However tired she was, duty triumphed.

John Wakeham, Chief Whip to Margaret Thatcher from 1983 to 1987 and Leader of the Commons from 1987 to 1989, was enormously impressed by her capacity for work. He wrote, 'Without exception, she was always the best-informed, best-briefed Minister around the table.'

He added in conversation that 'she always *had* to be the best briefed', which, while still impressive, is something a little different.

John MacGregor, who came into Margaret Thatcher's Cabinet in 1985 as Chief Secretary to the Treasury, corroborates John Wakeham's view in an anecdote in which he ended up the loser.

Before any meeting with Margaret Thatcher, you really had to do your homework – she did! The Chief Secretary had one of the most arduous workloads in my day, lengthy two-month negotiations with all Cabinet colleagues and spending departments on the annual public expenditure round, and constantly being brought in on any new policy initiatives or projects where extra public spending was involved. Not unusually, I took two red boxes home to work on overnight, and over weekends.

I remember one occasion particularly well. I had a meeting at nine o'clock the following morning at No. 10 to discuss with the Prime Minister and a few other Cabinet colleagues a particularly complicated project – one of the forerunners of what became known as Private Finance Initiatives, or PFI. I had a lengthy briefing meeting the night before in the Treasury, and took home a voluminous brief. By 1.30 a.m., I had completed the main brief with several appendices to go.

Margaret Thatcher had been at the Commonwealth Conference in the Caribbean for two exhausting days, then had gone on to New York to make a speech at the United Nations General Assembly. She was flying back overnight for our 9 a.m. meeting. I reflected that she would not have had time to go into detail, and went to sleep.

The morning meeting was going OK until she turned to me and said,

John, what about Appendix C? I hadn't a clue what was in Appendix C so let the discussion carry on while I quickly flipped through the papers to see what it was. She was right, it was the one issue I had queried without satisfaction the previous day with my officials.

I lost the battle. In all the mass of briefing, and after a punishing overseas trip, she had found my weak spot. She asked me to go back to the Treasury and think again!

Some of her close colleagues illustrate what I find a rather endearing trait in her character. She really did feel that never a moment could be wasted. The whole of her time had to be filled with activity, otherwise she would become uncomfortable and restless. This could happen during the briefest pause in proceedings – even if the occasions were important public ones. If there was a gap, she had to fill it by doing something useful, as Robert Armstrong, Cabinet Secretary from 1979 to 1987, recalls on the momentous occasion of the signing of the Anglo–Irish Agreement in Northern Ireland in 1985.

I accompanied her to Hillsborough in Northern Ireland for the ceremony at which the Anglo–Irish Agreement was signed by her and the Irish Taoiseach, Dr Garret Fitzgerald, on 15 November 1985. There was half an hour in hand before the ceremony began, and she and I, with Dr Fitzgerald and my Irish counterpart, Dermot Nally, were waiting in a side room. The Prime Minister said, 'Well, Garret, we have half an hour to wait. I suggest we have a rehearsal. Dermot can ask me all the difficult questions that the media will be

throwing at me, and Robert can do the same for you.' And that is exactly
what happened.

John Major describes a Whips' dinner in the House of
Commons where, in June 1985,

Margaret bustled in with Denis and, with drink in hand, discussed
the day's events in Parliament. We sat down for dinner, amid small
talk that bored Margaret even before the soup was served.

To say that she was easily bored is disproved by her appetite for the driest and smallest of detail in a brief. What
she could not bear was the waste of valuable time. As she
herself said, 'Every minute of the day has to be filled with
useful occupation,' a lesson learned in Grantham and
observed for the rest of her life. And as she wrote in her
memoirs, constant activity could be a welcome distraction
from other worries.

The account by Elizabeth Cottrell that follows illustrates
graphically the way Margaret Thatcher approached a task:
with concentration, attention to detail, professionalism
and enormous energy. Elizabeth had joined the Centre for
Policy Studies in 1980, where she was Director of Research
until 1984. She then became Special Adviser to Richard
Luce, Minister for the Arts and for the Civil Service,
and then my own Special Adviser at the Departments
of Employment, Agriculture and finally Education (then
Education and Employment) until 1997.

The Centre, founded by Margaret Thatcher and Sir Keith Joseph in the late 1970s, was known in the press as 'Margaret Thatcher's Private Think Tank'. By 1980, she was its Patron. We worked closely with the No. 10 Policy Unit, but the Prime Minister herself had naturally become somewhat distanced from our day-to-day activities. However, Alfred saw her regularly, often on Sundays, and would ring me in the evening with any relevant details from their meeting.

On Sunday 18 July 1982 the usual call came through, this time with a difference: 'Alfred Sherman here: I'm speaking from No. 10. The Prime Minister would like to talk to you. She hopes you can help her with a difficult speech. Here she is.' As I trembled with shock and fear, the familiar voice took over. It was an interesting assignment. Dame Margery Corbett Ashby, the co-founder of the Townswomen's Guild, had died in 1981, aged ninety-nine. The Guild had established an Annual Memorial Lecture in her memory and invited the Prime Minister to deliver the first one, on Monday 26 July. Dame Margery, born in 1882, had been a suffragette and a pioneer of social and educational reform – not what popular opinion would have called a 'Thatcherite'.

Mrs Thatcher explained, clearly and crisply, what she wanted – a consideration of the century covered by Dame Margery's life – the changes it had seen and the underlying verities which had not changed. I saw that a great plus in working for her would be that she seemed to know exactly what she wanted. Her concluding remarks explained why I had received this surprising request. 'Alfred tells me that you're an authority on the nineteenth century.' A gross exaggeration, but my PhD had involved a study of Victorian social reform. 'None of the drafts I have had so far have quite caught the right tone. Could you produce one for me? I'll have all the papers sent round in the morning and I would like the draft here by Tuesday 20th please.'

And that was that. I found the papers on my desk the next morning, and worked frantically. The draft went in as requested and I was summoned to see the Prime Minister on Friday 23rd at 3 p.m. This was a good sign, I was assured by Ian Gow, Mrs Thatcher's Parliamentary Private Secretary: she wouldn't even be seeing me if the draft was impossible.

I arrived promptly to begin one of the most amazing twenty-four hours of my life. The Prime Minister was moderate in her praise: 'You've worked very hard. You've done what I asked you to do. As a skeleton, this has possibilities. I think we can build on it.' She fingered another draft on the table and tossed it aside contemptuously. 'Not like this effort from the Research Department. Do they really think that I can preach party propaganda on an occasion like this?'

My spirits lifted. This suggested that I had got the right tone, but I prepared myself for similar trenchant criticism.

To my surprise, there was none. From the moment we set to work it was a joint effort, two people engaged in a common quest to perfect this speech. Mrs Thatcher obviously had a well-tried way of working. Each of us had a copy of the draft, while another was laid out, page by page, on the floor. It was to be a lecture, so was longer than most speeches. There were, at this stage, about thirty sheets. The Prime Minister had already marked where she wanted transpositions, expansions or contractions, or facts and figures to be checked. As amendments were made, a Garden Girl was summoned to take the pages down, section by section, for typing and re-typing.

Mrs Thatcher gave her attention to every detail, yet was always keen to ensure that the main theme, constant change occurring against the background of eternal truth, ran consistently through the speech. She would read and re-read to make sure that each page achieved that balance. Her painstaking approach was tinged with an unexpected dry wit.

There was considerable trouble from the IRA in 1982 and I had mentioned the fact that in 1882 the Chief Secretary for Ireland had been assassinated in Phoenix Park, Dublin. 'I'd better not say that,' she said. 'It would sound as if I want something to happen to Jim Prior.' (Jim Prior was at that time Secretary of State for Ireland, and a leading 'wet'.) Even though some of my favourite references were taken out, Mrs Thatcher was genuinely interested in them. There was a hymn by John Addington Symonds: 'I haven't seen that since Sunday School, however do you know it?' she exclaimed. The Prime Minister's intellect showed itself in her appreciation of the research and her insistence on factual accuracy. There was nothing shallow in her approach – not a whiff of 'the line to take' so dear to many, lesser, politicians. Then there was her Flaubertian concern for the 'mot juste'. The thesaurus was much in use. I saw how she moulded the text into her own style, using, for example, the technique of repetition. When read cold, this can seem banal, but in oration it makes the words memorable.

This meticulous process took a very long time. In those days I lived in Huntingdon, and by around seven o'clock, I began to wonder if and how I was going to get home. Clearly, this was not something with which to bother the Prime Minister. At some convenient moment, I thought, I would suggest that I went across to the Horseguards Hotel to book a bed.

I was forestalled. With a sigh of satisfaction, after finishing a difficult page, Mrs Thatcher said, 'You're not going to be able to get home tonight. You must stay here.' My feeble protests about the hotel were summarily dealt with. 'Nonsense! We've still a lot to do and I need you.'

Apart from the Garden Girls, we had seen no one for about four hours. Now staff started to come in to say goodnight. One was asked to make sure that towels were put out for me, another to get something out of the fridge for our dinner. I assumed that there was a housekeeper, lurking somewhere, to prepare the meal. But at around eight o'clock, it was the Prime Minister who went into the kitchen to cook the chicken supreme. Afterwards we washed up together.

Conversation was surprisingly easy. We talked mostly about books and poetry and interesting aspects of the nineteenth century which had arisen from the speech. Then it was back to work. At some point Carol dropped in and was asked to make sure that her room was tidy, because I would be sleeping in it. Mark, who was staying at No. 10, came in to say goodnight.

On we went, draft following draft. We were both now in stockinged feet, with a drink to sip: whisky for her, gin for me. The tireless Garden Girls came and went.

Finally, at 3 a.m., Mrs Thatcher decided that we should stop – until the next day.

There could be no better illustration than this account of Margaret Thatcher's ferocious industriousness, her energy, her tenacity and her determination to get things right for a particular audience. The lecture was, after all, not for a United Nations audience in New York, but for the Townswomen's Guild in London. Moreover, it was celebrating aspects of social policy with which most commentators would have assumed she was not in sympathy. It was appreciatively received by the audience. It is difficult to avoid a comparison with the totally disastrous and condescending misjudgement Tony Blair applied to a similar occasion, the Annual General Meeting of the National Federation of Women's Institutes in early June 2000. His slick and shallow approach earned him a derisive slow hand-clap from the 5,000 or so women assembled to hear him in the Royal Albert Hall, resulting in such unlikely headlines as 'WI gives Blair hostile reception' (BBC News, 7 June 2000). It has gone down in political folklore.

Some of the content of the Thatcher speech for the Townswomen's Guild, though (as opposed to its composition), is perhaps more questionable. It contains the sentence 'I hated those strident tones we hear from some Women's Libbers', a phrase not yet forgotten in feminist circles. The speech is included in full in the Appendix.

Margaret Thatcher believed strongly, and as a matter of principle, in keeping in touch with all sides of the parliamentary and voluntary Conservative Party. She therefore insisted that time was put aside in her prime ministerial diary for regular meetings with party officials and members, and for constituency matters. Anyone who has held ministerial office will know what a struggle it can be to continue to honour regular engagements with people outside the purview of the civil service, but she continued the practice until the end of her career. Even from the small sample of those who have contributed to this book, it is amazing to note how many had, and indeed expected to have, regular meetings with her. Observation of her successors, with the exception of John Major, forces me to conclude that they did not and do not necessarily follow her meticulous example.

Hazel Byford, a Conservative Women's Area Chairman in the 1970s, met biannually with the Prime Minister at No. 10, and more frequently when she became a member of the Conservative Women's National Committee and a member of the National Union. Joan Seccombe, who became a Party Vice-Chairman for Women in 1987, was 'far more regularly involved with her, having one-to-one meetings, as well as taking others to see her'. John Taylor had regular meetings with the Prime Minister 'as was customary for colleagues who were officers in the National Union, the voluntary side of the Conservative Party'.

As a new backbench MP, Janet Fookes had close contact with Margaret Thatcher.

When I entered the Commons in 1970, as a former teacher and Chairman of an Education Committee in local government I was much interested in education, and soon became an officer of the Party Education Group. I was truly surprised and pleased by the fact that Margaret, despite her many duties as Secretary of State for Education, thought it important to keep in touch with the officers of the group and instituted regular meetings with us to discuss the issues of the day. So far as I am aware, this was unprecedented while in office. I thought it was a real mark of her willingness to engage with backbenchers.

Henry Plumb, a former Chairman of the National Farmers Union and, for a period, leader of the British delegation to the European Parliament, met Margaret Thatcher every two weeks to give her an update on European issues. John MacGregor as Chief Secretary to the Treasury met her each week to brief her on Treasury matters. Robert Armstrong, her Cabinet Secretary, had one-to-one meetings every Friday morning.

John Wakeham, as Chief Whip from 1983 to 1987, took the parliamentary business managers to have lunch with her at No. 10 every Monday when Parliament was sitting, and attended almost all the meetings she held with ministerial colleagues. He points out that 'Mrs Thatcher sometimes held four or five Cabinet Committees in a day, and I was usually present', yet another regular commitment which had to be fitted in.

Even the hairdresser came regularly, three times a week, arriving early in the morning at No. 10. Once the television cameras were allowed into Parliament, it was more important than ever to Margaret Thatcher that she should look well-groomed at all times, and so to the weekly hair appointments were added regular comb-outs. Some of her male colleagues used to say that she greatly valued her conversations with the hairdresser, welcoming them as a voice from the real world.

The people who have contributed to this book give only a small sample of the fixed and regular commitments she expected to honour, in addition to the enormous weight of prime ministerial obligations. To their examples have to be added the innumerable meetings, visits, travel and fixed parliamentary and media appearances that filled her life. Margaret Thatcher was well known for needing only four hours of sleep a night, as Hartley Booth points out. But she set a standard for stamina and hard-focused work not equalled by any of her predecessors or successors.

TWO

'NEVER FORGET, DEAR, THAT IT IS THE *DETAIL* WHICH IS IMPORTANT.'

These were the words used by the Prime Minister when appointing me to my first ministerial post, that of Parliamentary Under-Secretary in the Department of Social Security, at a Downing Street reception in July 1989. She added, 'This is the post I started in, as you know, and it is a very important one.'

I was overwhelmed to the point of speechlessness. I then realised that I was meant to say something in response, so I asked what I should do next. 'I would get round to the department very early tomorrow morning, and make a good start,' was the reply. Naturally, I obeyed this to the letter, arriving at the DSS just after 8 a.m., to find cleaners in possession of the building and no sign of other ministers or officials. I returned to my office, wondering if it had all been some kind of mistake, and that I had possibly had the shortest ministerial career on record, to find messages on my phone from No. 10, my husband, my agent and my constituency office, all asking, 'Where are you?' It turned out that the Prime Minister had phoned again that morning (as part of the official reshuffle procedure obviously), as she put it, 'just to make quite sure', and I, equally obviously, could not be found as I was loitering outside the DSS. Not the best of starts, but an example of how the Prime Minister found the time to dot the i's and cross the t's, even with the most junior of ministerial appointments.

This attention to detail was a characteristic of her working method not shared by all her male counterparts, then or subsequently; one for which she was frequently ridiculed by political colleagues, but one which nevertheless stood her in good stead throughout her career. This sense that it was 'the *detail* which was important', coupled with her astonishing memory, served her well as Prime Minister, within the Conservative Party and with the public, and of course in her constituency of Finchley.

It was something she had learned, and demonstrated, very early in her political career, to devastating effect. She was selected as Conservative candidate in the constituency of Dartford in January 1949. The seat was a hopeless one for a Conservative: the incumbent Labour MP, Norman Dodds, had an enormous majority of 20,000, and was both popular and charming. He was chivalrous and pleasant to his young challenger in their quite frequent encounters on public platforms. However, Mr Dodds soon learned to his cost, and in full public gaze, that on matters of fact his young Conservative opponent was on all occasions formidably briefed and prepared. Stories about her dazzling performances as parliamentary candidate in Dartford were still remembered and being retold by the late Bob Dunn, MP for Dartford from 1979 to 1997, and other parliamentary colleagues, when I arrived in Parliament in 1987. Apparently at one election meeting, she criticised an answer Mr Dodds had given to a question and he challenged her to do better. To his amazement she had brought to the meeting a large number of copies of *The Economist*, one of which she consulted there and then, to produce the correct answer. This must have been devastating for Norman Dodds. It certainly impressed the Dartford audience. It also impressed Members of Parliament who heard the story. Without exception, we felt that to take a supply of copies of *The Economist* to an election hustings, and then to have the sheer nerve to consult them, actually during the meeting, just to prove one's opponent wrong, represented a determination not to be bested and a thoroughness of preparation none of us could begin to match.

Unsurprisingly, this approach, and the contrast it afforded between her and her predecessors, terrified Whitehall when she became Prime Minister, although civil servants in the Department of Education had had to accustom themselves to the technique when she was Secretary of State for Education. Her Cabinet colleagues, and even those much lower in the pecking order like me, became accustomed to seeing her handwritten comments in the margins of ministerial papers from every department. In this she was a complete contrast to her predecessor, James Callaghan, who, while a good chairman, preferred to distance himself from the detail. She, on the other hand, frequently gave the impression that she thought nothing would be done correctly unless she personally saw to it.

Frank Field, who as Labour MP has held the seat of Birkenhead since 1979, further illustrates the point.

One aspect of her premiership never ceased to fascinate me. It was her exercise of power in part through a command of detail. On one occasion I saw her in the early evening of the same day on which she had returned from, as she so eloquently put it, putting some backbone into President Bush (Sr.). We met in her study in Downing Street. She was like a cat on a hot tin roof. I had never seen her so excited. She marched around her study, explaining how she had had to put backbone into the President (the time of her famous comment, 'This is no time to go wobbly.'). 'Prime Minister, please come and sit down so that I can talk to you,' I pleaded. However, the marching continued, as did the declamations. When she had exhausted herself, she stopped, and asked me what I wanted. I went through my small agenda, much of it concerning Cammell Laird [a major shipbuilding firm based on the Mersey], whose fate greatly affected my constituency. 'Is that all?' she asked. I replied that it was. The marching recommenced, and I left.

The meeting had excited me, affording for a brief moment a small ringside seat into what was quickly unfolding as the First Gulf War.

Its timing had been fortuitous, and the drama of Mrs T. marching to and fro before me, and up and down the sides of the room where I was sitting, remained vivid in my consciousness throughout the following day. Indeed, it so mesmerised me that I forgot to report back to my three colleagues in the Wirral, who were also active in promoting the interests of Cammell Laird within the government.

Two days later I saw David Hunt, MP for a Wirral seat and a minister in the government. 'Oh dear,' I thought, 'I haven't reported back to the other three on what Mrs T. had promised to do two evenings earlier.' I went to apologise. My opening words were cut short. 'I see you saw the Prime Minister,' was his opening remark. I began my apology again. Again it was interrupted. Each relevant minister had received a copy of the prime ministerial minute, and it had been copied to their Permanent Secretaries.

There had been no one else in the Prime Minister's study that night when I met her. She was high on octane following her meeting with the President. Yet, at some stage that evening, a minute had been dictated on what was said and agreed during our meeting, and had been sent out to colleagues and departments for action.

Frank Field had lobbied Mrs Thatcher before. On that occasion, he said he had expressed his annoyance to her political office, which was preventing him from seeing her.

My retaliation, I told them, would be to kidnap the Prime Minister, tell her that her office was a menace and were not only preventing me from seeing her but, much more importantly, many of her own political party. I arrived back at the Commons after a dinner where I had been bored to the point where my bones ached, but where the pain and boredom had been somewhat anaesthetised by a generous supply of drink. A note awaited me on the message board, announcing that the Prime Minister would see me that evening after the ten o'clock vote. Panic set in. I could not remember the agenda I intended to cover with her. Slowly my mind cleared. I voted quickly and went over to stand at the exit from the No Lobby. Mrs T. as usual was the last one out. She timed her exit so that colleagues wishing to lobby her could do so. 'Shall I follow you, Prime Minister?' I asked. 'People usually do,' was the reply.

As she swept out of the Lobby, I longed to be able to see her face. Despite all the reports depicting her as totally lacking in any humour whatsoever, she must, surely, have been smiling as I inevitably did what others did, and followed her, to the office the Prime Minister has behind the Speaker's chair.

As we sat down, Mrs T. asked what I wanted to drink, and I was offered a single option. I therefore asked for a very, very weak whisky. She, looking at Mark Lennox Boyd, her Parliamentary Private Secretary at that time, replied that she too wanted a very, very weak whisky, emphasising to the point of mimicry the stress I had put on 'very'. Two whiskies quickly appeared. One looked like almost clear water, the other as though it was neat whisky. Mrs T.'s hand, as the tray was lowered, thankfully grasped the far from transparent glass.

'What do you want?' was, as always, the opening gambit. We discussed Cammell Laird and a vacant deanery that she would shortly fill. The business was over before she had finished her drink. The Cammell Laird request would be followed up, but we remained divided over the deanery.

Michael Brunson, Chief Political Editor for ITN during the Thatcher premiership, describes an early encounter with Mrs Thatcher in January 1978.

There were, I believe, three words which anyone who worked with Mrs T. needed to learn, and learn fast – 'Do your homework!' It was a lesson I learned the hard way.

In January 1978, the then Leader of the Opposition decided, somewhat unusually in those days, to go out and campaign for a candidate in the Ilford North by-election. I had not long returned from a spell as the ITN correspondent in Washington, and had already been told that, when the general election came, I would be the reporter assigned to cover Mrs T.'s campaign. Having learned all too little about her during my spell in America, what better opportunity to get to know her better than to watch her in action on the campaign trail?

As it happened, the morning on which I chose to do so followed her appearance on ITV the previous evening, when she had been asked about immigration. She had spoken about the British character and said, 'If there is any fear that it might be swamped, people are going to react and be rather hostile to those coming in.' Overnight it had become a huge story, with, for some, uncomfortable echoes of Enoch Powell's 'rivers of blood' speech ten years earlier. Labour's Denis Healey accused her of 'stirring up the muddy waters of racial prejudice' and the Liberal Leader, David Steel, called her remarks 'really quite wicked'.

At a small and surprisingly poorly attended press conference in Ilford, I decided to question Mrs T. on the matter. Did she now regret having raised the immigration issue during the interview? Suddenly, what President Mitterand of France once described as the eyes of

Caligula swivelled sharply in my direction. Too late I realised that, like many a soldier before her, she regarded attack as the best form of defence. What on earth was I talking about? She had not raised *the matter. She had simply answered a question on the issue. How on earth could I be talking about her having* raised *it? Was it really too much to expect journalists to do their homework properly, as she always did?*

It was typical Thatcher. In some considerable political trouble, she had seized the opportunity which my loose use of language had given her to fight her way out of it. Over the ensuing thirteen years, I saw her use that tactic many times. Woe betide the sloppy journalist, or politician for that matter, who was ill prepared or badly briefed. They could expect a mauling or worse. I think I only slipped up on one other occasion, when, during an end-of-summit press conference in Bonn, I put to the then German Chancellor Helmut Schmidt a spectacularly ill-advised enquiry. Sitting beside the Chancellor, Mrs T. turned in the opposite direction towards her Press Secretary, Bernard Ingham, and in the biggest stage whisper you ever heard, declared, 'What a very silly question.'

In the year 2000, Mrs T. was kind enough to record a message for a farewell video my colleagues put together when I left ITN. There were good reasons, notably the abolition at the time of News at Ten, *why I decided to go, though she could not resist referring to my leaving 'at the early age of sixty'. She then added that I always seemed to know exactly what questions to put to her. She would, of course, have long forgotten our first encounter in Ilford twenty-two years earlier, at which she had delivered her stern admonitions about homework, but believe me, I never did.*

Virginia Bottomley was appointed Parliamentary Under-Secretary at the Department of the Environment by Margaret Thatcher in July 1987, with the words 'Never turn down the opportunity to explain the government's case; no one else will.'

> *After I settled in at the Department for the Environment, the Prime Minister developed an obsession with the evils of litter dropping. It was a wonderful example of her ability to take a relatively trivial subject as seriously as matters of international importance. I was summoned to Downing Street with my boss, Nicholas Ridley. Douglas Hurd, as Home Secretary, was also present. Lengthy discussions took place about whether penalties for litter dropping should be raised. I was despatched to Paris to study the operation of officials on motor bikes, freezing or squirting dog mess off the pavement.*

Virginia does not recall if she ever reported back after this trip, but many will remember press photos of the Prime Minister armed with a large black bag and a spiked stick clearing up rubbish in one of the London parks. 'We were afraid she wouldn't stop until she'd cleared the whole park,' one official said afterwards. Virginia continues,

> *Withstanding the challenges of the miners and the economy, Margaret Thatcher turned to broader environmental issues. As a junior Environment Minister, I was the lowest form of ministerial life at the 'Saving the Ozone Layer' Conference in 1989. I was the great lady's bag carrier. Hearing her interrogate officials in the green room*

before going on stage was a lesson. No detail, however awkward, was missed. That way she was confident she knew the answers and the questions. It was an example I followed.

Events, rather than career structures and formal appraisal, alter the course of political lives; do not expect measured career planning and development. As part of the ministerial fall-out following Nigel Lawson's resignation in October 1989, David Mellor was moved to the Foreign Office and I was summoned to Health. The Prime Minister's call was arranged at the Waverley District Council Office as I was about to start my surgery. 'You have done well at Environment, Virginia, we would like you to move to Health. You know all about that, don't you?' Ten minutes later, the reshuffle was on the news.

Testing arguments, policies and ministers to destruction was a feature of Margaret Thatcher's decision-making process. In 1990, the NHS reforms were to be approved. The legislation was due to be introduced in Parliament. Ken Clarke, the Secretary of State, Tony Newton, Minister of State, and Sir Duncan Nichol, our resilient and talented NHS Chief Executive, were summoned to Downing Street. I joined the team. The debate opened with the Prime Minister asking her adviser, at that time the successful businessman, David Wolfson, to comment on the plans. An intense, almost hostile, critique followed from him. But we survived, and the NHS reforms proceeded. If only more politicians thought through the implications of their initiatives with the same focus, preparation and attention to detail, we might achieve more.

Michael Brunson recounts in his book, *A Ringside Seat*, how Margaret Thatcher used her mastery of detail to devastating effect against political opponents – the same skill she had deployed against her first political opponent in Dartford, Norman Dodds.

> During a terrible day in the House of Commons for Neil Kinnock, I watched as she destroyed him by simply picking away at the facts. Then having won the argument against him, she turned witheringly to tell the House, 'I fear the Right Honourable Gentleman is not the master of his brief!' As very many people, not just in the opposition parties, or the media, but in her own Cabinet, government and party, were to learn, it was always a good idea to master your brief, and to master it to the letter, before confronting Margaret Thatcher.

John Campbell in *Margaret Thatcher* explains this obsession with detail as one of the lessons she absorbed from her father.

> She still prepared for parliamentary questions or international summits like a schoolgirl preparing for an exam. She was contemptuous of opponents, colleagues or fellow heads of government who had stinted their homework. But however much they had done, she always expected to do more.

As one of her Cabinet told me, 'She always knew more about other people's briefs than they did themselves.'

This inevitably led to a feeling across Whitehall, fully

developed by the time I became a junior minister in 1989, that the spirit of the Prime Minister was somehow every-where and in every department. Peter Hennessy, in his book *The Prime Minister*, describes it thus:

> This was the period which established new expectations of prime ministership – what one might call the stretched premiership of late-twentieth-century Britain. In William Waldegrave's judgement, we had 'not had such all-pervasive personal government since Churchill as a war leader: perhaps since Lloyd George as a war leader, since there were large areas of policy on the home front about which even Churchill did not much concern himself. There were no such areas under Mrs Thatcher.'

Geoffrey Howe writes,

> Her influence was deployed much more opportunisti-cally and instinctively than we should have planned. But throughout Whitehall and Westminster her instinct, her thinking, her authority, was almost always present, making itself felt pervasively, tenaciously and effectively.
>
> It came gradually to feel, as the months went by, as though the Prime Minister was present, unseen and unspeaking, at almost every meeting. The questions were always being asked, even if unspoken: how will this play at No. 10? What's the best way of getting the Prime Minister on side for that? And so on.

This is certainly how things seemed to me in my first ministerial post at the Department of Social Security in 1989.

Nothing could have been more crushing to a brand new junior minister than to be told, frequently, 'No, Minister, we cannot do that. It isn't government policy.' Eventually, I gained sufficient confidence to ask, from time to time, who made policy – ministers or civil servants. On the other hand, after eleven years of a government's life, the weight of the government's 'line to take' weighed heavy. What I should have realised at once was that the line to take was the No. 10 line.

While I was at the DSS, a furore arose on the level of war widows' pensions. We were bombarded with thousands of letters from MPs and others, pointing out the need for a rise and the inequity of the existing arrangements. In fact this was a Ministry of Defence matter and any increase would have to be paid for out of their budget. In the end, when the sacks of letters we had received on the subject had filled the post rooms, Tony Newton, the Social Security Secretary, took us, his ministerial team, at the dead of night from our Regency surroundings at the DSS across the road to the Stalin-esque MoD buildings, to consult Tom King, then Defence Secretary, and his advisers. I will never forget how we crept through the department, past dozens of brightly lit offices, all absolutely empty apart from uniform jackets hanging from the backs of chairs. Tony Newton, a heavy smoker, was suffering from nicotine withdrawal, and an unhappy man.

When finally we arrived at Tom King's sanctum, it was to be told by him, dismissively, and with an air of finality, that the MoD had received no correspondence on the issue – this seemed likely since we in the DSS had surely had all there could be. There would therefore be no change in policy. Mrs Thatcher's shade hovered above us. Paralysis set in. The two Secretaries of State looked at each other, and almost together said, 'No. 10 will never wear it, not to mention the Treasury.' So we crept dejectedly back to the Department, where I caused the normally mild-mannered Tony Newton to explode with rage as he was able at last to light up a cigarette by asking, 'Has anyone actually asked the Prime Minister? There is a genuine inequality in the current situation, which she would appreciate, surely, and we are going to get hammered by the tabloids. It is a perfect issue for them, and they will go on and on. And what shall we do when Vera Lynn gets involved, as she surely will?'

'You are the most junior minister in this Department,' he almost shouted. 'Don't think you can just make policy on the hoof because with Margaret Thatcher you can't.' He was obviously in an impossible position: he himself was convinced of the case; he was attracting all the flak, and was unsupported by colleagues. Meanwhile Armistice Day was approaching. Vera Lynn did get involved, and a media frenzy ensued. The Prime Minister was finally consulted. She agreed. Tony Newton said afterwards, 'We did at least avoid the involvement of the Queen Mother.' But I learned a lot from the episode, not least that with the Prime Minister, it was always worth making a case – provided of course that you had done your homework!

Hartley Booth describes what it was like to work for someone so ferociously hard-working and tenacious.

There was never a case of any note going to her that used three words where one was enough. I was expected to warn her of impending trouble, propose improvements to policy and to comment on briefings coming from my three Departments: Home Office, Environment and the Lord Chancellor. Other ministers and senior officials sent in material to No. 10. I was the cog that commented on everything relevant in my area if I felt it was necessary. How did Margaret receive her briefings from me and the Policy Unit members? Cartoon characterisation would have you believe it would be a brutal regime in No. 10 in which we all lived in constant fear of 'handbagging'. This was not the case. Until Margaret Thatcher's mind was made up, she was not just open to new ideas and proposals, she welcomed them. She listened intently and read with great focus.

Life was made easier by two things: there was an atmosphere of encouragement and we knew Margaret's policy principles. I, and indeed the civil service, responded best because we knew the goals and the framework or targets with which to work. Consequently policy had to be tested, for example, by applying the questions such as: 'Does the proposal produce value for money?'; 'Is it in line with the manifesto?' (I had the manifesto on my desk all the time.); 'Does it increase government control or reduce it?'; 'Could the proposal be regarded as nannying?'

Policy briefings and other reports would frequently enter the red boxes and in-trays of Ministers and stay there for far too long. With Margaret, you were always sure that papers put to her would be read speedily and marked assiduously. Her custom was to underline comments, and put ticks and crosses in the margin. There might be the occasional 'NO' beside a comment. Happy were the moments when a tick and an 'MT' inscription was put beside it. Things would then happen and sometimes very fast indeed. One proposal for example, that gained one of her 'yes, do it' ticks became legislation in just three months. (It resulted in the Sporting Events (Control of Alcohol etc.) Act of 1985.) This was at a time when the whole country had become appalled by the bad behaviour displayed at football matches. Margaret, with the proposal in front of her, and with strong support from Denis, saw to it that the legislative process was fast-tracked. When I told her a year later, 'Prime Minister, this season there are a third fewer reported football crowd crimes thanks, it seems, to the introduction of CCTV and control of alcohol on the terraces,' I received another comment in the margin: 'Excellent.'

One of the fascinating points about Hartley Booth's account above is his listing of the four criteria which had to be applied to policy proposals under Margaret Thatcher. With such a firm framework to work to, there is no wonder that the spirit of Thatcher seemed to float above every desk.

Ian Beesley, between 1981 and 1986, served in the Rayner/Efficiency Unit at No. 10. He describes first how he was appointed to the Unit and then, rather like Hartley Booth, how he found successful ways of working with the Prime Minister, despite the fact that he was a civil servant.

I was not long back from the cash limits division in Denis Healey's Treasury when the Thatcher government came to power. The Winter of Discontent had ended, but the civil service had goose bumps at the prospect of the threatened cold winds. Cash limits had been central to the control of expenditure following the 25 per cent per annum inflation of 1975, and during the IMF crisis of 1976. But the appointment of Sir Derek Rayner of Marks and Spencer as Mrs Thatcher's part-time unpaid adviser on eliminating waste was widely seen as a last chance for the civil service. If Rayner failed, said my Permanent Secretary, Sir John Boreham, expect the next appointment to be a Genghis Khan.

Thatcher was determined, it was put to me, to tame the jungle of official statistics, and I was to be the lead statistician member of the team to do so. Twice I said 'no' to the career-limiting appointment, finally to be drafted on the authority of the Head of the Home Civil Service, Sir Ian Bancroft. Other promising young civil servants were similarly chosen to carry out the Rayner 'test drillings' of the value for money from typical departmental activities (known as scrutinies). They reported directly to their Secretaries of State with recommendations which, largely unheard of previously, carried the names of those responsible, which were produced to a tight timescale and which were not to be amended by the departmental hierarchy. This was 'close up and personal' on a new scale.

It was during that first assignment that I realised that though Mrs Thatcher disliked the civil service, she appreciated individual civil servants and especially those whom she perceived were trying to change things for the better.

At the end of 1980, Rayner rescued my career by appointing me general manager of the scrutiny programme. I learned how to make submissions that would stand a fair chance of gaining Mrs Thatcher's agreement. All but the most trivial would be read personally, and phrases that made an impact on her, for good or bad, would be underlined in felt pen. Short notes, in an unmistakeable, slightly elaborate handwriting, would instruct the relevant Private Secretary what was to be conveyed on her behalf. The skill, I soon discovered, was to keep things brief, to deploy evidence in support of the arguments and above all to use language which would resonate with her – stick to concrete examples and avoid the woolly abstractions so often encountered in 'management speak'. There was another reason. All those who lead units for a Prime Minister must speak from time to time with the voice of their master, and the recipient must not be able to tell whether the words come directly out of his or her mouth, or are interpretations of what he or she would have said in the circumstances.

Evidence mattered, and we soon learned to deploy it effectively. 'Give me an example', was a frequent response to a statement or suggestion. If satisfied, Mrs Thatcher would let the conversation move on, and then when least expected would return to probe again. 'What you said about X was very interesting,' she would say. 'Have you another example?' Success in her cross-examination depended upon having evidence in depth, and being able to deploy it as the discussion zigzagged forward. Thus, she ensured that she controlled the flow of argument and that you stayed focused.

This fascinating account demonstrates Margaret Thatcher's revolutionary role in introducing, through the Rayner Efficiency Unit, a complete change in civil service working methods, in that those responsible for producing papers were also held accountable for them. This does not seem so revolutionary now, but the absence of such a principle before does go some way to explain Mrs Thatcher's exasperation with the civil service practices she had encountered on her arrival in Whitehall. Ian Beesley also illustrates Mrs Thatcher's own approach to accountability. Her insistence on detail, and on fully understanding the practical detail of a proposal, meant that she knew that she herself would have to explain and be responsible for it at the despatch box, and, thereafter, to the public.

At other times, such as opening the October 1985 seminar on management responsibilities for junior ministers, her deep belief that management in government mattered shone out, perhaps, in hindsight, at the risk of appearing patronising. 'You have been appointed to get results, not just to hold office' and 'Getting results out of the department is the mark of a minister in the driving seat' were part of her opening remarks. Few would have been persuaded but all would have registered the rules, and for those of us working to give effect to good management as a policy in its own right, to hear her say so unequivocally that our efforts were important and valued was inspirational. However, when she addressed a question to me, in front of everyone, to check if what a Permanent Secretary had just said was accurate, for me was somewhat fraught with danger!

It was through this combination of looking for the evidence firsthand, seeking the underlying causes and having a plan for practical action that working for Mrs Thatcher brought home to me the opportunities I had and the enduring loyalty I owed to her. It was a five-year rollercoaster ride, at once exhilarating and frightening and never to be forgotten.

Margaret Thatcher's approach to politics was that of one who sought solutions to particular problems rather than the discussion of abstract principles. As Ian Beesley says, she regarded a successful minister as one who got results. She would always ask how a policy would work. So much the better, surely, since government's policies affect everyone's lives. It is curious that this practical approach to politics, the constant question 'how will it work', which characterised much of her domestic policy, somehow failed when it came to the poll tax, where despite the model process of consultation, Green Papers and White Papers, and a full process through the relevant Cabinet Committees, the wrong decision in the end was taken.

Margaret Thatcher's tireless attention to detail paid great dividends in her contacts with the public, who were invariably impressed by the trouble she had taken to inform herself about them as individuals. Janet Fookes recalls that

on one occasion I had a visitor to the Commons from Australia who expressed a great wish to meet her. Margaret explained that she would not be able to meet him until after the ten o'clock vote. The division having duly taken place, Margaret kept her word, and chatted with the visitor, taking a lot of time to talk to him and showing an amazing knowledge of the construction of the roof of the Sydney Opera House. The guest was astonished (and so was I) that late in the evening she showed such kindness and knowledge to someone simply passing through.

Hazel Byford writes,

Her clarity of thought combined with her ability to work long hours made her a remarkable adversary and a good friend. As Prime Minister, she set the standard and would expect from others the same commitment. The Conservative Women's Area chairmen used to meet the Prime Minister once a year, when we would be asked to give a short resumé of the issues affecting our particular area. The best piece of advice I was given for these occasions was to think of the supplementary questions that might be raised from my contribution. Her single-mindedness, the ability to listen and seek clarification are skills I have always remembered, and they have remained through my parliamentary life. I did not consider her approach overpowering, but one was certainly on one's mettle on these occasions.

Mrs Thatcher was an inspiration whether talking within a small group or giving her end-of-conference speech – she was totally engaged. Many who neither shared Conservative policies nor were admirers of our leader would openly admit that even so, she was an amazing lady. But there was much more to Mrs Thatcher than was publicly recorded, and that was her detailed concern for others on a personal level. I share but one such example.

In 1985, Val Pulford became Chairman of the East Midlands Area Women's Committee, but she was also a member of the Leicestershire County Council and the North West Leicestershire District Council, both of which were 'hung'. This workload proved too great for her, and she stood down after her first term as East Midlands Chairman, although she continued to work tirelessly for the party for over thirty years. She never received any public recognition for this work. In 2002, I had the chance to raise this with Margaret Thatcher, who responded with a personal handwritten letter to Val. Val said that in retrospect she often thought that she was more a Thatcherite than she was a Conservative. Mrs Thatcher's influence is well known, but many of her detailed and individual kindnesses are not so well documented.

John MacGregor was startled, sometime after he had left his post as Chief Secretary to the Treasury, to be introduced by Margaret Thatcher to a visiting overseas Finance Minister at a reception as the former Chief Secretary who had told her the role 'was one of the jobs he would have most wanted'.

I was amazed. I was not sure she had even heard what I said at the time, let alone remembered it all those years later!

John Alston became the Leader of the Norfolk County Council in 1981, a post which he held until 1987, and then again from 1990 to 1994. He recalls a political visit by Mrs Thatcher to Norfolk in August 1981.

After I became Leader of the Council in May 1981, Michael Heseltine, the Environment Secretary, announced changes to the Rate Support Grant system which had disastrous consequences for rural authorities. In effect, his system rewarded high-spending authorities, and penalised the low-spending ones, like Norfolk. The Association of County Councils organised a special meeting at their headquarters of officers to plan their response. One of their number leaked the time and place of the meeting to Michael Heseltine, who turned up uninvited and unannounced, but inexplicably armed with a blackboard, with the aid of which he proceeded to bombard us with an impromptu presentation. He spoke well, but with scant regard for the facts. At the end of his presentation, I stood up to deliver a tirade of the true facts, and a protest that he had somehow appeared at what had been intended as a private meeting. Naturally, this was leaked to the press, where I reinforced my view of Mr Heseltine. There was widespread national and local coverage.

About a fortnight later, I received a call from the South Norfolk Conservative agent, asking if I would be prepared to host a luncheon for Mrs Thatcher at County Hall on 6 August. I said I would, provided I got twenty minutes on my own with her, which was agreed. Originally it was intended to be a private political visit; she did not wish to meet the Lord Mayor of Norwich or the Chairman of the County Council. I was to go and meet her at Norwich Airport. Eventually she was persuaded to meet the Lord Mayor – anything less would have been a severe slight – and the District Council Leaders.

I had seen Mrs Thatcher before, but it had been at a huge Conservative rally during the 1979 election campaign. On this occasion she came straight down the steps of the plane and walked over. I remember the characteristic walk, not inelegant, but purposeful. She was strikingly good looking, immaculate hair and clothes, and above all, a wonderful complexion, flashing eyes and warm smile.

She began by test-driving some Lotus cars round the airfield, where she met John MacGregor, MP for South Norfolk, at that time Minister for Small Businesses. She then visited a factory making modern kitchens, gave a press conference, and an address to the party faithful at a local dance hall. I attended all these events. Even from a distance, you could see she gave all those she met her absolutely undivided attention.

We eventually arrived at County Hall, where our private meeting took place in the Chairman's room. She admitted straightaway that the Department of the Environment had got the Rate Support Grant policy all wrong, but she would not be saying so today, there would be a statement in the autumn. She then changed the subject, and asked to be briefed, in detail, on the concerns of fruit farmers, whom she would be meeting that afternoon. Their problem, in particular affecting apples and blackcurrants, was the effect on their profits of cheap fruit imports from France and Poland.

She was in very good form over lunch with the District Council Leaders, light-hearted gossip about a recent visit to Egypt, but mostly I remember her flirting with Eddie Coke (Viscount Coke, at that time the Leader of the King's Lynn and West Norfolk Council), with long discussions about his family history, which she either knew or had been briefed on.

After lunch she did a brief photo call with the County Council chairman and then a photo opportunity on the steps of County Hall, instructing me to turn left, while she turned right, to give the press and people watching from the windows a good picture.

I had a very nice letter of thanks from her, and in the autumn I had a call from her office to say that Michael Heseltine would be making a statement in Parliament that afternoon about adjustments in the Rate Support Grant. Someone somewhere ran a very efficient office. She had said that if I ever had any other difficulties I should be directly in touch with her office.

Some considerable time later, the County Council was having problems in getting a Bill through Parliament to set up the Broads Authority. We were opposed by the Port and Haven Commissioners, the MPs, who were either against or sat on the fence, and other special interest groups of various kinds. The Bill was declared hybrid. That had the advantage of being able to survive the dissolution of Parliament, but equally, it had to be in the party manifesto at the forthcoming election. I did not trust Conservative Central Office to deal with this, so Hartley Booth arranged a meeting in her private apartments in No. 10. She came in, brightly, and just as I remembered, proffered a large whisky, listened carefully, asked a few questions, and left. It did appear in the party manifesto of 1987, and became law in 1988.

Nothing could be more characteristic of Margaret Thatcher's approach than this account by John Alston. If she was convinced by the detail of a case, she would act – and action followed. The Broads Authority Bill was a case in point; not that important politically, but it needed to be correct, well-supported and, above all, workable. Because of her personal attention to it, it was all of those things.

Incidentally, the Norfolk visit provided an illustration of the Prime Minister's technique with political demonstrations. A number of demonstrators had gathered outside County Hall, and a couple of obviously official cars swept in, taking all the tomatoes, eggs and shouted abuse prepared by the waiting protesters. Her car then followed at speed, before the protesters had time to re-equip. This method never failed, and I recommended it to French colleagues, notably Martine Aubry, and my agriculture counterpart Jean Puech, who were obsessed by the potential embarrassment of enduring a demo with a British colleague sitting alongside them in the official car. History does not relate if they ever adopted the practice.

Margaret Thatcher's attention to detail, and in particular her prodigious memory, were perfectly suited to the role of a constituency MP. Even now, when I meet people who were her constituents in Finchley, they will recall her work for them, the fact that she knew their names, and the names of their children, and called the rabbis by their first names. She continued to hold regular surgeries throughout the whole time she was Prime Minister, despite the obvious implications for her security, and I have been told many times of the occasion when she walked a mile in the snow to the inaugural meeting of the Finchley Friends of Israel.

In many ways, the Finchley constituency might have been made for her. She had, of course, twice fought and lost elections in Dartford. Jean Lucas, a Conservative Party agent, recalls inviting her to address a supper club in the Norwood constituency, in the hope that it might help her in her search for a seat. She tried and failed to get selected for Orpington, Beckenham, Maidstone and Oxford. But Finchley, where she was selected in 1958, and which she represented until she left the House of Commons, was predominantly middle class and aspiring in character. Owner-occupiers were the largest group. Twenty per cent of the population were Jewish. At the time of her selection, there was a safe Conservative majority of 12,000.

In *The Path to Power*, she describes how she prepared for the selection process. 'Like any enthusiastic would-be candidate, I set to work to find out all there was to know about Finchley.' By the time of the initial interview for the seat, she had briefed herself on the issues likely to be of concern to local people: rent de-control, immigration and the economy.

> I had voraciously read the newspapers and all the briefing I could obtain. I prepared my speech until it was word-perfect and I had mastered the technique of speaking without notes. Equally important was that I should put myself in the right state of mind, confident but not too confident. I decided to obey instructions (from Donald Kaberry, a senior party agent at Conservative Central Office), and wear the black coat dress. I saw no harm either in courting the fates, so I wore not just my lucky pearls but also a lucky brooch which had been given to me by my Conservative friends in Dartford.

All this had the desired result, and she duly became the candidate.

Then, of course, came the preparation for the general election.

Finchley had been run with a degree of gentlemanly disengagement that was neither my style nor warranted by political realities. I intended to work and then campaign as if Finchley were a marginal seat, and I hoped and expected that others would follow my lead. From now on I was in the constituency two or three times a week, and regularly went out canvassing in each of the wards, returning afterwards to get to know the Party activities over a drink in the local pub or someone's house ... By the time the election was called in September 1959, the constituency was in much better shape, and I had begun to feel very much at home.

Hartley Booth, Mrs Thatcher's successor in Finchley, writes,

At the end of July 1991, I was selected to be Margaret's successor. Technically of course I was selected to be the Prospective Parliamentary Candidate for the constituency of Finchley. It was all over the world press and I urgently needed to liaise with her, the sitting MP, to ensure that I did not make any politically unsound statements to the media, who were literally queuing up to discover what it was like to follow the great lady. She came on the phone and said, 'Congratulations.' Then she said, 'Can you afford it?' As with so many areas, Margaret was concerned about matters of detail and so often thinking of the people around her, sometimes in the most disarming way, like this. It was one of the reasons I could never abide the mindless hectoring she suffered, and that I too received from the left, that she did not believe in Society. She believed in society with a small 's', which meant the Christian principle of loving your neighbour, and she certainly believed in community, not leaving it all to those who provided from the great height of Whitehall, but as neighbourly actions of getting involved in the nearest charity, or in voluntary work to help people around you.

She did not believe in the individual as a selfish autonomous unit, either. She sees the individual as a person with dignity and responsibilities towards neighbours. 'Selfish greed' was the mindless accusation against Margaret and her policies. Nothing was further from the truth.

These conclusions came from my encounters with her over the two stages of my work with her. I was overwhelmed by the evidence of the love and care she had shown to constituents over the years, extending from the local special school for children with autism to the many dozens of constituents I met.

Before the election, Margaret briefed me on the needs of the Greek Cypriots and the Jewish community. She took a judicious stand on the latter group, very properly avoiding backing any one political party in Israel, and stressing that the country should observe UN rulings with regard to its neighbouring states.

The constituency party members revered her. One man was papering a wall in his house with her written replies to his questions. (He continued with mine until I put a stop to it.) People told me how she would organise her arrivals to be exactly on time. They would say, 'Prime Minister Thatcher was a wonderful MP. We could always rely on her punctuality. If the car bringing her was early, we would see it go round the block, and park. Then on the dot, her driver would stop outside the hall or wherever, and out she would step. We thought she was royalty really.'

Harvey Thomas was Director of Presentation at Conservative Central Office for thirteen years from the late 1970s onwards. He writes, 'My relationship with Mrs T. not only crossed between government and party,' as he puts it,

> but as it happened, by the time Marlies and I were married in 1978, we were also Margaret's constituents in Finchley, and remained so throughout her time in power. This gave us, of course, yet another perspective. I doubt if her many friends in the constituency would claim it for themselves, but Mrs T. was enormously strengthened by the total loyalty and support from her constituency leaders, together of course with her constituency secretary, Joy Robilliard. The support from the constituency was superb, led in later years by her agent, Mike Love. I remember many times in Downing Street or some other official location in different parts of the world, when her eyes would relax and you could sense her pleasure as she referred to constituency friends and what, in many ways, she regarded as her 'real' foundations in Finchley.

Sir Donald Stringer, the senior Conservative agent responsible for the London area for much of the whole period Mrs Thatcher was a London MP, recalls how he would receive phone calls from her from all over the world, if word had reached her that something was not going well in Finchley.

Finchley played an important part in Margaret Thatcher's first election as Leader of the Conservative Party in 1979. Doreen Miller explains:

*The first occasion I had any connection with her was when, as the new
Leader of the Party, she was preparing for her first general election, in
1979. Mr Callaghan was deferring it for as long as he could. As an
activist in the constituency adjoining hers, I was asked to secure contributions and to edit a pre-election (and pre-election expenses!) leaflet
which was produced with the considerable assistance of a local journalist, Dennis Signey, in the form of a newspaper which we grandly
called* The Finchley Leader. *Its first headline read 'We will be the
next government.' Mrs Thatcher was able to make considerable use of
this paper in the run-up to her historic victory in 1979.*

She certainly did. The paper gave regular reports of
her activities as opposition leader, of her speeches in the
Commons and her policy announcements, and national
journalists came to regard it as authoritative enough to
repeat and quote in their newspapers on a regular basis.

Cynical political commentators almost invariably ignore
the constituency element of a politician's life. But there is no
truism more certain that you get back from a constituency
what you put in, in terms of effort, presence and attention
to detail. If Margaret Thatcher, at difficult moments, felt
supported by Finchley, that is because Finchley knew that
every detail of its collective and individual life mattered
to her.

THREE

—

'THERE WAS ALWAYS A LITTLE DANGER ABOUT HER, APPREHENSION OF A DAMNING PUT-DOWN OR MEMORABLE ERUPTION.'

Margaret Thatcher's ferocious attachment to hard work, her high standards and stamina, her insistence on getting things right, had a flip side. She could be impossible to work with, given to tantrums, tears and shouting matches and lightning changes of mood. She was indeed, as John Major says, 'a woman of contrasts who could behave with great kindness, yet who was equally capable of great intimidation'.

Throughout her leadership, Margaret Thatcher was portrayed in the press as confident, battling, principled, unwavering, domineering, arguing, occasionally losing, more often winning. She was an extraordinarily divisive figure, and remains so to this day. Very few people are neutral about her, and the mere mention of her name still arouses strong reactions, not only in Britain, but also abroad.

In opposition, and in her first parliamentary term as Prime Minister, however, there is plenty of evidence that she was privately much more hesitant than her manner indicated.

In *One of Us*, Hugo Young describes how

alongside the euphoria [of the success of the 1979 election] went anxiety... None of her colleagues had ever experienced a more assertive, more overbearing leader ... in part it was an act put on to convince herself and others that she really was the boss.

Those who were in a position to observe Margaret Thatcher at close quarters confirm this initial lack of confidence.

Matthew Parris, who worked in her private office in the early days of her leadership, and was later a Conservative MP and then a journalist, puts it thus:

History, having concluded that Margaret Thatcher was a tremendous, convinced, directed and unstoppable force, has all but forgotten the fragile self-confidence, the hurt, the panic, the changeability and the near despair that, I keep having to remind myself, I saw in the early days. ('A time, a place, Two entirely different stories', *The Times*, 26 May 2012.)

This hesitancy was also noted by Michael Jopling, her Chief Whip from 1979 to 1983.

Although I did not actually hear her say it, I know that when she took over as Leader of the Opposition she did say that one problem was that all the brains were among the right wing of the Conservative Party. She also described Keith Joseph as her muse. It has surprised me that if that was her view then, she must have changed it before 1979, when she appointed a Cabinet with a strong left-of-centre flavour. As a result she failed to get Cabinet support in 1980 for the economic policy proposed by her and Chancellor Geoffrey Howe. So, in two shuffles in 1981 to restore the balance, she dropped Christopher Soames, Ian Gilmour, Norman St John Stevas and Mark Carlisle. But what surprised me was that her muse Keith Joseph never held any of the great offices of state, Treasury, Home Office or Foreign Office.

She almost fell into the same trap again in 1982 when she had another shuffle. At a very late stage when all was agreed, we pointed out to her that she was again poised to appoint a Cabinet which had a similar slant to the earlier one. As a result of this, changes were made to redress the balance. Among other changes, she brought in Lord Cockfield as Trade Secretary at the last minute.

Given that of all the members of a probable Cabinet after the 1979 election, only two, Keith Joseph and Norman St Stevas, had voted for her in the leadership election, it is hardly surprising that she was at first hesitant of making wholesale changes to her Cabinet. The fact was that the Conservatives were divided after the 1979 election. In a way, she was there on sufferance, not least because she was a woman. There was a great deal of male muttering and covert joking. She must have been aware of it, and it cannot have been conducive to confidence in her own leadership. Jim Prior was not the only one of her colleagues who found it irritating to be led by a woman. 'I found it very difficult to stomach,' he later wrote.

There is no suggestion that Patrick Cormack, at the time MP for Cannock, shared Jim Prior's distaste for a woman Prime Minister. On the other hand, he reflects the ambivalence towards Margaret Thatcher, on policy grounds, within the parliamentary party. Not only was she a woman, but she was taking the party into policy areas to which it was not accustomed, and to priorities not necessarily shared by colleagues.

I was of course aware of Margaret Thatcher as a rising star in the Tory ranks, when, as a very young schoolmaster, I fought the impregnable Labour stronghold of Bolsover in 1964, and even more so when I contested my home town of Grimsby eighteen months later. I had heard her speak at Party Conferences and candidates' gatherings, and there was much talk of her being in the next Conservative Cabinet. The first time I was really conscious of her as a force to be reckoned with was when she was in charge of Education in Ted Heath's government of 1970, when my victory in Cannock, against another formidable woman politician, Jennie Lee, helped put the Conservatives back in power. Margaret quickly made her mark at Education, and not just as 'Margaret Thatcher, milk snatcher'. From my point of view, as someone who had been educated at a grammar school, and taught at one, it was a disappointing mark, for there was no attempt to roll back the engulfing tide of comprehensive education, no clarion call for the virtues and values of the sort of school from which both she and I had benefited.

I did not find it easy to be a fervent backbench supporter of the first or indeed the subsequent Thatcher governments. It was partly because she herself never seemed to be fully in sympathy with the needs and aspirations of manufacturing in the Midlands, where the first three years of the Thatcher administration did not go down well. There is certainly little doubt that hers, like Ted Heath's, would have been a one-term government had it not been for the extraordinary events of April 1982, the invasion of the Falkland Islands.

My biggest falling-out with her came during her second and third terms, over her decision to abolish, rather than reform, the GLC. There was no sustainable case for depriving London of a directly elected local government, and I said so, and voted accordingly. And then, of course, there was the Community Charge, the 'poll tax', where I was one of only two Tories who refused to support its experimental introduction in Scotland and who consistently voted against it thereafter. So my relations with the woman I had helped to elect to leadership of our party were sometimes a little difficult.

While Patrick Cormack expresses no personal antipathy towards the new Prime Minister, and certainly no objection to her on grounds of gender, these views, many of which were shared by parliamentary colleagues, illustrate just how precarious was Margaret Thatcher's position in the early days of her first government. Her reaction was emphatically not to betray any insecurity she may have felt, but rather to become, on occasion, overbearing and difficult.

John Major, as a former Chancellor and Foreign Secretary in a Thatcher government and eventually her successor as Prime Minister, was very well placed to observe some of the personality issues.

In the years since she left office, Margaret Thatcher has been buried under myth. The real Margaret – the one I knew, and for whom and with whom I worked – was more studied, more pragmatic and far more interesting than the stereotype celebrated in a thousand half-truths and exaggerations. I hope history records the reality and not the caricature. She was a woman of contrasts who could behave with great kindness, yet who was equally capable of great intimidation. I experienced both these character traits first-hand in the mid-1980s when I was appointed a Treasury Whip.

At a Whips' dinner in June 1985, Margaret, accompanied by Denis, was becoming increasingly bored by the pre-dinner chat. John Wakeham, the Chief Whip, accurately reading Margaret's impatience,

silenced the room, saying, 'Let's begin', and went on to state that, given Treasury policy was crucial to all our plans, the Treasury Whip should brief the Prime Minister on the current concerns of the parliamentary party.

I obliged, but perhaps too vividly. I told the Prime Minister that the party was not enamoured of our policy. In fact, many of our members disliked it intensely, and were openly saying so in the tea rooms. Only loyalty was holding back their discontent and that was already being stretched to breaking point. We were close to facing a rebellion.

'What exactly are they concerned about?' came an icy voice from across the table, as her soup went cold. Unperturbed, I set out a detailed list, most notably that colleagues believed that worthwhile capital expenditure (which they favoured) was being sacrificed to sustain current expenditure – especially on social security (which they did not favour). Every Whip present had heard the same complaints on a daily basis, but they seemed entirely novel to the Prime Minister, and entirely unwelcome.

Margaret was livid and began attacking me as though the views I had reported from the party were my own. Her reaction was so wildly over the top that my fellow Whips studied their empty soup bowls and shuffled uneasily in their seats. Infuriated by the injustice of her behaviour, I reiterated that it was the job of a Whip to report the party view whether the Prime Minister liked it or not. Unsurprisingly, this did not calm her mood.

Carol Mather – ADC to Montgomery – intervened to support me. So did Bob Boscawen, blown up in a tank and terribly scarred. These were two of the bravest men I have ever known. Margaret slapped down Carol and glared at Bob. The temperature continued to rise. Jean Trumpington, a Lords Whip, attempted to diffuse the situation but had her head snapped off. It was an extraordinary scene, which significantly delayed the main course until we eventually, and uncomfortably, moved on to other issues.

At the end of the evening, the Deputy Chief Whip, John Cope, whispered in my ear that I 'might care to make peace with the Prime Minister'. I did not. I was still seething at the injustice of her attack on me and others.

Yet the very next day, this extraordinary woman of contrasts came to sit beside me on the front bench, where I was the Whip on duty. All warmth and smiles, she suggested we continue our discussion in the Whips' Office. I talked. She listened. All was sweetness and light. Three weeks later, she appointed me Junior Minister at the Department of Health and Social Security. 'It's a good job,' said Margaret, 'It's where I started.' And so it was. This was not the only disagreement I had with Margaret, but it was certainly the most memorable.

In the furore of that Whips' dinner in 1985, I learned something crucial about Margaret's modus operandi: *she did not like people who were pliant. She liked a good row and thrived on it. Indeed, going into battle often helped her reach a decision.*

Working with Margaret was always challenging, but equally stimulating. When she was in agreement with you, she was as forceful in support as she could be in opposition. Moreover, if she felt comfortable with you, a great deal of latitude was offered before your opinion was challenged. This was one of the reasons why she attracted such strong support from almost all those with whom she worked.

Like all iconic figures, Margaret Thatcher attracts stories which are an absurd travesty of the truth to those who know her and wish her to be fairly and accurately represented. And those of us who know her owe her no less than she expected from us: the unvarnished truth – not least for the sake of historical record.

Harvey Thomas provides an interesting explanation of Margaret Thatcher's behaviour:

Margaret has a clear and simple approach to friendship. She has said many times, 'Friends are there to be taken advantage of – and I expect them to take advantage of me.' This was both a strength and a weakness, because sometimes her unwavering belief that you could say anything and do anything to 'trusted friends' could have negative consequences. I think her approach comes from an openness that for the most part is straightforward, but could occasionally leave the wrong impression.

On the positive side, in 1981, the late playwright, Ronnie Millar, John O'Sullivan and I, and Mrs T., were sitting in No. 10 working on a speech. On one section, I made the comment, 'I don't really like this bit.' 'Don't you, Harvey? What would you put in its place?' I hadn't thought through any further than an initial negative reaction to the section, and I stuttered, 'Er, er, er, well I, er...'

'For goodness' sake, Harvey,' she exploded, 'I've got a country to run, and we've got to finish this speech. If you don't have anything better to suggest, let's get on with it.'

Of course I was chastened, to say the least, and tucked my head down to let Ronnie Millar do most of the talking for the next few minutes. But it was not even five minutes later when she turned and said, 'What do you think about this, Harvey?' as though there had never been a cross word.

As we left the room, Ronnie Millar turned to me and said, 'Well, Harvey, welcome to the family.' I asked him what he meant, and he said, 'Well, you do realise she would never have raised her voice to you unless she regarded you as a trusted friend.'

I had only been working with her for two or three years, and those words were spoken privately in a small group, but they still ring proudly in my ears more than thirty years later.

Robert Armstrong was Secretary of the Cabinet from 1979 to 1987. Margaret Thatcher appointed him in a typically decisive manner, on 9 July 1979.

I was of course no stranger to her. I had come to know her and see something of her when she was Secretary of State for Education in Edward Heath's administration and I was his Principal Private Secretary, and I had had occasional meetings with her on security-related matters when she was Leader of the Opposition. So I went to 10 Downing Street with a cautious hopefulness when I received a summons to go and see the Prime Minister.

I was disconcerted when the first thing the Prime Minister said when I went into her study was, 'Robert, you're looking very tired.' It was a worrying opening to a meeting at which I hoped that I was going to be invited to take on one of the most onerous positions in the civil service. I mumbled something about having been up rather late the night before, and then the Prime Minister said, 'Robert, I want you to succeed John Hunt as Cabinet Secretary when he retires in October. I should like you to know that I have not thought of asking anyone else.'

How could I have done otherwise than gratefully to accept an offer so generously expressed? So I went downstairs and told the Principal Private Secretary that the Prime Minister had offered me the job but that it had been a little disconcerting when she started by remarking that I was looking very tired. He laughed, and said, 'Oh, you don't need to worry about that, she's saying that to everybody this morning.'

That was the introduction to eight fascinating and action-packed years of working for and with Margaret Thatcher, whom I invariably addressed as 'Prime Minister'.

Every Friday morning at 10 a.m., I would go for my weekly meeting with her to discuss and plan the business for Cabinet and for Cabinet Committees of which she was chairman, for the ensuing three or four weeks. If she had other engagements that morning, our meeting would be short and business-like. If she did not, our meeting could go on far into the morning, and we would talk about many other things.

On one such occasion the Prime Minister wanted to discuss a memorandum I had recently submitted to her. She was clearly not persuaded by the recommendation I was making, and she argued quite fiercely, like an advocate (she had been a barrister), testing and contesting my case. After a time, I heard myself say, 'No, Prime Minister, you're wrong.' I wondered if I had gone too far and whether that was not how one should address a Prime Minister. I remembered what Queen Elizabeth I said to Robert Cecil. 'Must? Is "must" a word to be addressed to princes? Little man, little man! Thy father, if he had been alive, durst not have used that word.' But the Prime Minister paused, and said, 'Why do you say that I am wrong, Robert?' I had burned my boats, and so I said why I thought she was wrong, chapter and verse, facts and figures. She did not interrupt me, and when I had finished, she said, 'Thank you, Robert, you're quite right. I was wrong.'

This incident did wonders for our mutual respect. I knew that she would listen and could be convinced. She knew that I would not put something to her which was not properly thought through. But those discussions were to be had only unter vier augen. *I thought that it was not my business to argue with her in that way at meetings when her colleagues were present.*

Henry Plumb recounts a rather similar experience. After nine years as President of the National Farmers Union, from 1970 to 1979, he was elected to the European Parliament, subsequently becoming the President of the Parliament in 1987. It was in his capacity as Chairman of the European Committee on Agriculture that he had regular meetings, every two weeks, with Margaret Thatcher in the early 1980s.

On one occasion we met late at night following a successful vote in the Commons, to discuss the European issues of the day. She greeted me very warmly and we had an extremely amicable conversation, accompanied by three large whiskies. As I was leaving, her mood suddenly changed, and she said, quite belligerently, 'Henry, we must discuss the Common Agricultural Policy. I am not *going to put any more money into the pockets of these peasant farmers in France, and elsewhere in Europe.'*

I must have been emboldened by the three whiskies and I found myself saying, 'If you will just shut up for one minute, I will tell you about the CAP.' Not surprisingly, she looked a little startled at my less than tactful words, and said, 'You'd better come back in.' So we went back into her room, more whisky was provided, and I said, 'Those peasants as you call them, the small farmers, get nothing out of the CAP. It is big farmers like your brother-in-law, on his farm in Essex, who are getting the money from the intervention payments they receive on their surplus wheat, £50 a ton while we still have a wheat mountain. Yes, the CAP wants changing, but surpluses are not the fault of the so-called European peasants, their problem is social, not economic.'

Her jaw dropped. 'How do you know my brother-in-law?' she asked. 'I was on his farm only last week,' I said, 'and I can tell you that what I said is right. You can ask him yourself if you want.'

I never again heard her blame 'European peasants' for the problems of the Common Agricultural Policy, but I always wondered what kind of conversation she might have had when she next saw her sister and brother-in-law.

I left without being handbagged.

[Margaret Thatcher's sister, Muriel, was married to John Cullen, a farmer, in 1950, and they settled in Essex.]

Ian Beesley describes an episode in No. 10 where handbagging did occur – with somewhat negative results.

Her tendency to lead from the front has been well reported. It left colleagues and officials in no doubt about the direction in which her mind was turning, and that was important in helping officials think about options. But it could bring trouble. I was present when Michael Heseltine presented his Ministerial Information System (MINIS) in a slide show in a first-floor reception room at No. 10 in 1981. Throughout, John Nott, Secretary of State for Defence, conspicuously worked on departmental papers, demonstrating his indifference to Heseltine's initiative. Nothing daunted, Mrs Thatcher started the question-and-answer session with, 'I can see that the Secretary of

State for Defence has been taking copious notes throughout, so perhaps he'd like to begin.' He did so with telling words, 'My Department is different, Prime Minister...' The invective that followed from the Prime Minister, and directed at John Nott [for so obviously ignoring the presentation and then opposing its arguments], *wrecked any chance of others sticking their heads above the parapet, and with it, the prospect for widespread adoption of MINIS.*

John Taylor, as an officer in the National Union, the voluntary side of the Conservative Party, had regular meetings together with his colleagues with the Prime Minister in No. 10, which were often unpredictable.

Shortly after the time of the tenth anniversary of her premiership (in May 1989), we were seated in Downing Street for one of these gatherings. All was going fine with conventional, even deferential, questions, when my friend and colleague John Mason asked a question about Europe. He raised it in terms which implied that the Conservative Party and the electorate needed a clearer indication of what government policy was on the issue.

What then followed was a display of verbal pyrotechnics which was glorious to behold. The then head of the EU Commission, Jacques Delors, came close to being described as a 'little H' which was aspirated away only to emphasise what she thought of the Commission's President. Whether she was right or wrong to take such an aggressive approach to John's question, it certainly gave us a glimpse of the political energy which made her such a powerful conviction politician.

Janet Fookes, while impressed by Margaret Thatcher's charisma and hard-working approach, was taken aback by her strong, and possibly irrational, reaction to the name of a distinguished educationalist whom Janet mentioned during a conversation with her.

> The effect on Margaret was immediate. It was not so much that it struck a chord but rather that it ignited a fire. She made it plain that she did not trust him at all and that nothing that he said would be of any interest to her. She did not explain why she had come to this view and frankly it did not seem politic to enquire further! It was, however, an indication to me that she felt very deeply about people, whether for good or ill.

Michael Jopling, who as her Chief Whip from 1979 to 1983 was in a position to observe her closely, writes,

> It has often been said that she talked too much and interrupted her colleagues too often. I think this did become a problem in the later years, causing some resentment. But I have strongly resisted suggestions that she would not listen to the views of others. She was open to listening to new proposals, but she wanted to be both convinced herself and at the same time to be sure her minister was able to argue his case in the face of her own cross-examination. Often I heard her say, 'Well, Secretary of State, you had better get on with your proposal. But if it goes wrong, don't come back to me to sort it out.'

She found it hard to dissemble, in which respect she did perhaps differ from the popular perception of a politician.

Michael Jopling describes a meeting with Canadian Premier Pierre Trudeau.

Argument was meat and drink to her. I shall never forget a very small lunch with Pierre Trudeau ... whom she did not admire. He had similar feelings about her and the verbal fireworks on a series of world issues were, what she described about another of their meetings, 'lively'.

John Wakeham, who succeeded Michael Jopling as Chief Whip,

very soon learned that if she took a letter out of her handbag it was not just important, it contained views she instinctively felt were right. On the rare occasions she was wrong, I always felt I was more likely to get her to change her mind if I set about it slowly and with a little subtlety.

One example was when she wanted to write a letter which I felt was unwise, so I suggested that because the letter was so important, she should get a senior official to look at the drafting and tighten it up if possible. He was sent for, and after a good go at this, I suggested that as the letter was likely to leak to the press, it might be a good idea to get a press adviser to look at it. He was fetched, and after he had given his rather forthright views, the letter idea was abandoned and a more successful approach was adopted.

My first serious encounter with her was when I was a Minister of State at the Treasury. I had made some rather radical tax proposals which she did not like too much, and she sent for me. I felt my political career was about to end before it had really begun. I determined that my best course was to stick to my guns and keep smiling! After a long debate, she said, 'All right, John, we will do it your way, but you had better be right. Let's have a drink.'

Sir Richard Parsons, whose long and distinguished Foreign Office career included three ambassadorial posts, was well aware of Margaret Thatcher's attitude towards civil servants and the Foreign Office when, as Leader of the Opposition, she visited the European Security Conference meeting in Belgrade in 1977. Sir Richard was the Leader of the British Delegation to this important body, a position he was given because, he says, the Foreign Office wanted someone 'emollient' to fill it. They were obviously right; his account illustrates that a little guile, and a gently humorous approach, could work wonders with Margaret Thatcher.

Mrs Thatcher came out to see how I was performing. As Leader of the Opposition, she was cheered to hear that I was a poor feeble creature. She thought that this might be a good opportunity to smack at the Labour government. To her surprise, we got on quite well at a dinner given on her first night in Belgrade by my British colleague, our ambassador to Yugoslavia. Next morning she sent me a friendly note saying how much she had enjoyed our meeting.

I sprang into life and made a few quick telephone calls to diplomatic colleagues from the Conference, and secured agreement that I should be called upon to speak that morning. I then, of course, invited Mrs T. to hear a specimen of my oratory. We proceeded to the

Conference Hall, where she took a place behind me, arousing much interest among the colleagues. As privately planned, I was soon called upon to speak, and made a robust speech about human rights, denouncing in particular the poor performance of the Soviet Union. At the conclusion, Mrs Thatcher congratulated me warmly, saying that I had spoken well.

As we adjourned for morning coffee, the effect of all this was slightly marred by the behaviour of our Russian colleague, an able man called Vorontsov. We were on quite good terms and sometimes lunched together in discreet seclusion. On passing Mrs Thatcher and myself, Vorontsov somewhat spoilt the effect of my efforts by giving me a satirical wink. Fortunately, Mrs T. did not seem to notice. On her return to London, she notably refrained from attacking me in the House of Commons. The Foreign Office were relieved and pleased. Shortly afterwards we were transferred to Madrid, where I served for four-and-a-half busy years from 1980 to 1984. This period encompassed the Falklands conflict.

The Spanish Prime Minister, the able Calvo-Sotelo, had the sense to see that Mrs Thatcher could be an ally in getting Spain into the European Union and NATO and thus into democratic Europe. He helped us in various discreet ways which made a favourable impression. The time was right to try and make progress over Gibraltar.

The trouble was that the Franco regime had closed the frontier between Gibraltar and the Spanish mainland. This was a great handicap to our side. If we could get the barriers removed, it would be much easier for Britain to support the return of Spain to the modern world. The advantage would be to both sides and under the leadership of our excellent Foreign Secretary, Lord Carrington, we agreed to draw up and submit to ministers a draft agreement which should do the trick. Calvo-Sotelo was to visit Downing Street for this purpose.

On the morning of the day itself, I flew to London and arrived at No. 10 to find Mrs T. holding a briefing meeting with Lord Carrington and his officials from the FCO. I slipped into a modest place at the end of the table. The PM was saying that she was very unhappy about the draft agreement. It gave too much away, she thought, and would not be acceptable to the Conservative Party. I cleared my throat noisily. 'What's that noise you are making, Ambassador?' snapped the Prime Minister. 'I was trying to control my amusement, Prime Minister.' 'Amusement?' echoed Mrs T. in a voice worthy of Lady Bracknell. 'Perhaps you would care to explain.' 'The truth is, Prime Minister,' I replied, 'that this morning I saw off the Prime Minister of Spain at the airport in Madrid on his way to London. I heard him telling his officials the same thing as you. The draft would not be acceptable to his party.'

'The Spanish Prime Minister is worried too, is he?' responded the Prime Minister, with marked satisfaction. 'That's the first piece of good news I have heard today.'

Everything was then smoothly agreed on our side. Afterwards Lord Carrington said to me very kindly, 'You arrived just in time.'

I learned something from this episode. Mrs T. had the reputation for being bossy and opinionated and averse to listening to both sides. But it was more complicated than that. She liked to hear both sides of an argument, properly explained to her. She would listen carefully if you knew your facts and were not afraid of deploying them. Heaven help you, though, if you tried a fudge. Then she would come out firmly on the winning side and present it to the world as if it were the only possible option. The Iron Lady was privately amenable to reason.

How else could she have remained Prime Minister for so many years?
But the public never quite spotted that and imagined that she became
a kind of dictator.

One might assume that Margaret Thatcher's aggressive style would prevail at any meeting with the trade unions. But this is not how John Monks, describing himself at that time as 'a "bag carrier" who accompanied the then TUC General Secretaries, Lionel Murray and Norman Willis, to critical meetings with her at times of national crisis', writes of a meeting at No. 10 in 1981, following the inner-city riots.

How times – and the power of the unions – change. In 1981, following the riots in Bristol, Brixton, Toxteth and Moss Side, when important parts of our cities were ablaze and tensions ran high, the TUC could demand and secure a meeting, not just with the Prime Minister but also with all her senior Cabinet colleagues with economic responsibilities. The situation was deeply disturbing. It felt like our civilisation was collapsing, as TV relayed dramatic shots of violence, looting and fires. Our purpose was to use the riots to press the government to act decisively on unemployment, which was up near the 3 million mark, and especially on youth unemployment and inner city dereliction.

A delegation from the TUC General Council therefore met around half the Cabinet in 10 Downing Street.

Mrs Thatcher was not the dominatrix on this occasion. She farmed out our various points to William Whitelaw, Geoffrey Howe,

Michael Heseltine and others, obviously a pre-arranged tactic to lower the temperature. Not that it worked with the TUC. We are more comfortable with the broad brush than the technicalities and the meeting ended with nothing. But Mrs Thatcher was, on that occasion, the courteous diplomat, far from the fierce warrior against the unions that later became the dominant judgement of history.

However, on a later occasion, John Monks writes that the

harder side of her was more obviously evident during the Miners' Strike of 1984–5, that year-long bruising battle with the strongest union in the country. It was a disaster for the miners, their families and their communities.

The TUC had been working hard to support the miners' families but particularly to find the basis for a settlement. With Norman Willis, I was one of those, along with ACAS, who shuttled quietly between Arthur Scargill and government ministers and civil servants in a vain attempt to find a settlement.

The culmination was a request from the TUC to meet the Prime Minister with a formula to end the strike. In truth, the strike was ending. Miners were going back to work in increasing numbers and the South Wales men, the most solid, the most loyal of the loyal, wanted an organised return. We all knew that, so did Mrs Thatcher. We wanted a deal which would at least be a basis for rebuilding relationships. We needed a face saver for the miners and a basis for a resumption of normality.

But at that meeting, Mrs Thatcher was adamant – no more talks with the NUM, they must return to work forthwith, they must accept the closure of the pits. There was no generosity, no quarter, no echo of Churchill's 'in victory, magnanimity'.

It was also a signal that the TUC as a whole was being relegated to a less influential role. The Iron Lady was emerging from this conflict as she had from the Falklands War, confident in her own judgement and determined to win her battles with her presumed enemies.

I am not a paid-up member of the Mrs Thatcher fan club.

I acknowledge fully her clear leadership, tactical skill, and a powerful executive ability to get things done her way, all admirable qualities in a Prime Minister, and qualities which mark her out as an exceptional Prime Minister. She put her stamp on the country and no one was in any doubt about what she wanted. That is a hallmark of effective leadership.

John Monks, as an experienced leader and negotiator, is able to recognise these qualities in someone with whom he had profound policy differences, as he goes on to explain.

But I disagreed profoundly with the direction she took, while admiring her executive drive to achieve her ends. As time has passed, many of her causes have been shown to have failed the long-term interests of the nation, although they were short-term triumphs.

The North Sea tax revenues were spent on tax cuts for those in work – a formula which worked brilliantly in electoral terms but left us with little to show for the great opportunity for national renewal that was offered by the exploitation of North Sea oil.

Council house sales were another brilliant political manoeuvre, but the problem of providing housing for those who cannot afford to buy is worse now than it was in the 1980s.

Privatisation of the utilities has been widely copied abroad but many now are in the hands of overseas companies and none of the remaining British ones have emerged as global or European brands.

And what of liberalisation of financial markets? Mrs Thatcher presided over the 'Big Bang', the deregulation of the financial markets. In 2008, we learned to our cost the huge downside risks of this. The burden of returning the banks to normality and paying off our debts will last for another generation.

And in my own backyard, the trade unions. Mrs Thatcher is widely acclaimed for her determination to take on and vanquish militant trade unionism, 'the enemy within'. But in this battle there were many casualties, especially in the north of England, Scotland and Wales, and the inner cities. And the long-term effects are now clear: a major loss of manufacturing capacity and a rise in inequality as boardrooms have felt less constrained and have paid themselves salary and bonus increases unjustified by performance.

And finally, in taking a Eurosceptic stance, she missed the need, which has existed on and off since 1870, and is very evident today, to build our economy more on German lines, with excellent manufacturing, high savings, long-term thinking, high skills, and job security, worker participation and high standards of corporate governance. If only she had deployed her undoubted executive ability on these goals, what might we, and she, have achieved?

Patrick Cormack also regrets lost opportunities.

I have absolutely no doubt that she will go down in history as a great Prime Minister. She was an international statesman of great calibre.

She curbed the power of the trade unions and transformed British industry in the process. Her privatisation policy rolled back the frontiers of the state and became the example for nations around the world.

But on constitutional issues she displayed little vision or understanding. She was wrong to abolish the GLC, but she was wrong on Scotland too, and wrong in a very big way. And I do not just mean treating Scotland as a guinea pig for the introduction of the poll tax.

The Callaghan government fell following the two devolution referendums in Scotland and Wales. People tend to forget that in Scotland there was a majority in favour of devolution. It was just not a big enough majority to cross the threshold that Parliament had, very sensibly, decided to impose, but there was a real need to recognise the concerns of the Scottish people and some of us put to her that it would be sensible – remember that this was in 1979 – to have the Scottish Grand Committee meet, not in Westminster, but in Edinburgh and Glasgow and other Scottish cities, too, and to do so on a regular basis. There was also a case put to her to have a consultative group of heads of local government and other leaders from Scotland, with whom she would meet once a year. She would have none of it. And I well remember in 1996, chatting over a whisky with Donald Dewar. 'What would have happened if we had done something like that in 1979?' I asked him. 'You would have shot our fox,' he replied.

Finally, Margaret refused to grasp the need to make changes in the House of Lords. It seemed to me, and to many others, that a Second Chamber which was largely hereditary, and where that hereditary element was almost entirely Tory, was not something that would survive a Labour government with a decent majority. Far better to have a system, taking the Acts of Union of 1707 and 1801 as precedents, whereby the hereditary peerage elected so many of their number to sit in the House each Parliament, and to create a situation where no party had a massive built-in majority. I even introduced a Private Member's Bill on the subject in 1984 but, again, Margaret would have none of it.

I often think that had she shown the same degree of foresight, determination and courage over constitutional matters as she did over foreign affairs and the domestic agenda, the history of the last twenty years would have been very different.

As John Major points out earlier in this chapter, myths about Margaret Thatcher's style of government, and in particular, her disagreements with ministerial colleagues on policy issues, have abounded since she left office. The three accounts which follow, from John Major, Douglas Hurd and Lynda Chalker, dispel some of those myths about very particular policy differences and events.

John Major writes:

Perhaps surprisingly, when I was Chancellor, we never disagreed about entry into the Exchange Rate Mechanism, although we frequently discussed it.

Neither of us wished to enter a single currency but, like Nigel Lawson before me, I saw the ERM as an anti-inflation mechanism and, albeit reluctantly, Margaret saw the logic in that. She hated inflation, which was reaching towards 10 per cent, and had no other option available to bring it down.

When she and I eventually agreed that Sterling must enter the ERM, she was enthusiastic in discussing the timetable (which was brought forward) and the political tactics of entry. If she had any reservations she never shared them with me. Legend puts out an absurd notion, that Margaret was 'bullied' into entering by Douglas Hurd and me. This is, of course, risible. No one would have been able to 'bully' Margaret into anything, even if they wished to try. She always gave as good as she got, which was both her strength and her weakness.

Douglas Hurd, Home Secretary and then Foreign Secretary to Margaret Thatcher, recalls the myth of the handbag:

Like most famous people, Margaret Thatcher is surrounded by myths; in her case the myth of the handbag is one of the strongest. She is supposed to have used the handbag as a receptacle for all kinds of secrets with which she backed up her habit of interfering knowledgeably while she was Prime Minister in the affairs of every department. My own experience was the opposite, at least when I was Home Secretary between 1985 and 1989.

There were several matters in the Home Office portfolio about which the Prime Minister felt passionately, but she hardly ever intervened and by and large left me to carry on as best I could in what she recognised as a difficult job. For example, she never once in five years suggested that the government should make a move to restore capital punishment even though I knew that would be her strong preference. On the whole she left me alone, only complaining mildly when something happened to surprise her, for example a prison riot. Provided she was spared such surprises, she backed me strongly in Cabinet.

Things changed when the Prime Minister moved Douglas Hurd, 'somewhat against her will', to the Foreign Office, where

> *the scene somewhat altered, but this was inevitable. For ten years, she had been deeply immersed in foreign affairs; she knew the people with whom she had to deal, both on the British side and overseas. I got used to her occasional outbursts against her fellow Europeans, but these were usually reserved either for the attempts to brief her before a meeting, or for the press conference or Commons statement after it was over.*

Lynda Chalker held ministerial posts at the DHSS, Transport and the Foreign Office in Margaret Thatcher's governments. Her views on Europe and on South Africa diverged from those of Margaret Thatcher, but in her account it is clear that those differences were of a greater magnitude in the collective eyes of the press at the time than in her view of the Prime Minister, either then or now.

> *When Mrs Thatcher became our leader, like so many other women in the Conservative Party, I was excited, and determined to help her make it to Prime Minister. Having long been a keen European, I was well aware that there would be some difference of opinion and approach, but having always seen the Conservative Party as having a broad spectrum of views, I was determined to do my bit.*
>
> *The first chance came when she appointed me a junior opposition spokesman on Health and Social Security in November 1976. Getting*

to grips with pensions and social security was a formidable task, which she well knew. It was thus always heartening to have her quiet enquiries, and later, when I was a minister, her remarkable support. Once we were in government in that department, we all worked the ministerial machine to try to turn round MPs' enquiries and also to reform policy so as to keep the ever-spiralling budget under control and to rid the system of the incredible contradictions in entitlements.

It was in 1982, when we were legislating to remove strikers' benefits, that I knew of her full support. The Minister of State on the Social Security Bill Committee, Hugh Rossi, had a heart condition, and could not work after 1830 hours, so when debates went on, first in the Commons until 2200 hours and then in Committee through the night, with a timetable motion in force to deter the Labour opposition from their continual filibustering, I was on my own leading the government team. The most controversial part of the Bill was the removal of strikers' entitlement to social security. The opposition put down a wrecking amendment and we began to debate it at two in the morning! Within minutes of the start of the debate, the public gallery door opened, and in came the Prime Minister with a Private Secretary to listen. She remained with us for the full two hours the debate took, and wrote me a very kind note once we had defeated the opposition amendment.

There were many times when I was Minister of State for Transport when the Prime Minister gave quiet but firm encouragement, such as the battle to have seat belts made compulsory to save lives. Many backbenchers thought that this was anti-libertarian and so opposed the law change, but the Prime Minister gave me her full support to introduce the government-agreed measure, which has *since saved many thousands of lives and prevented much injury in road accidents.*

From the day I went to the Foreign Office in 1986 to work on Europe and Africa, I knew that my real political battles would increase. In fact, the Single European Bill to get rid of trade barriers and establish much improved working with our European Community neighbours was exactly in line with our manifesto commitments, but it was at about the time when some outrageous statements from M. Delors of France and Signor Andreotti of Italy began to inflame the anti-European fever among a proportion of our backbenchers. Throughout the passage of the Bill, I had nothing but active support from Margaret.

Later, our views on Europe diverged, but there was rarely a time when I felt I would not be supported, and Margaret was the very person who had given me the real chance in politics to focus on Africa, the development of which has been my interest and concern since I helped two girls from Botswana back in 1955. While I was still Minister of Transport, I was encouraged by her to develop transport exports in Africa, and work in West Africa had encouraged me to sharpen up my conversational French. Thus as Minister for Africa from 1986 onwards, I had the chance to expand my interest and to help to resolve many issues, thanks to Margaret Thatcher.

Our views may have differed, but many discussions allowed me to learn a great deal from her and her colleagues in committees and Cabinet when I attended in the Foreign Secretary's absence overseas.

The early years of Margaret's premiership were very tough at times, but that was the time when the foundations of many reforms were laid. Even if we differed, as our experiences in life were so changed by our exposure to the very challenges we had been elected to solve, I shall always be grateful for her advice and friendly guidance, so often given quite unexpectedly.

All three – John Major, Douglas Hurd and Lynda Chalker – were able to achieve a *modus operandi* with the Prime Minister, even though they did not share all of her views. The accounts also indicate that, on occasion, she was prepared to listen and accommodate difference in order to make progress. But there is too much evidence of her over-ruling objections from colleagues and, on occasion, simply shouting them down, actually in Cabinet, for it to be ignored.

John Hoskyns, in *Just in Time: Inside the Thatcher Revolution*, analyses it thus:

> She did not seem to understand that colleagues could not answer back without being disrespectful, in front of others, to a woman and to a Prime Minister. She was too ready to blame others when things went wrong, and gave too little praise or credit when it was due. None of these things would be forgiven when her position became weaker.

In particular, the aggression she showed towards Geoffrey Howe, despite the many years they had worked closely together, seems inexplicable and, indeed, inexcusable.

In his book, *Conflict of Loyalty*, Geoffrey Howe describes an extraordinary incident in December 1981 as he prepared to make his Autumn Statement to the Commons. Compared with the events that led to his resignation, this episode ended relatively well although the description of the Prime Minister's behaviour is, to say the least, unedifying.

Howe realised that 'this particular exercise (the Autumn Statement) was almost bound to be a public-relations zero, at best. For its essential structure lacked virtually all the tax-cutting or scene-shifting components that can add cheer or authority to a proper Budget.' In the event, the press and public reception of it was much as he expected, with the *Daily Mail* describing it 'as electrifying as an algebra lesson'.

He continues,

But the most startling treatment of my Statement came from next door, in the form of a last-minute row about the presentation. The Prime Minister had been closely informed about, indeed engaged in discussing, the substance of everything that I had to say, and had not objected. But when, on the day before the Statement's delivery, she was routinely sent the full text, she protested vigorously. She delivered this presentational broadside (and she was right about the problem though short of a solution) at an early-evening meeting with me. This led me to summon a group of senior advisers and drafters to a late-night meeting in the downstairs sitting room at No. 11. We met at about 9 p.m. Some were in favour of sticking to the original text, John Kerr and some others were for revision, if only on the ground that it would be politic to make at least some changes.

We were still at work on this exercise when we were interrupted (and astonished) by the arrival of the Prime Minister through the connecting door with No. 10. Margaret had apparently just returned from a dinner engagement (I never did find out where), and been told by her Treasury private secretary, Michael Scholar, of the meeting taking place next door. To his dismay, she decided to join the proceedings. We had no time to think of reducing the large cast present. Margaret, who was in most unprepossessing mood, proceeded to play to the gallery outrageously, more than I had ever witnessed before. Anyone who attempted to describe the reformulations on which we had agreed was shouted down. So was I. At one point she exclaimed, 'If this is the best you can do, then I'd better send you to hospital and deliver the Statement myself.'

The storm eventually blew itself out and the lady withdrew. A shaken handful of trusties stayed on to complete our redraft. Michael Scholar and John Kerr prudently decided to withhold the product from Margaret until the morning after. It was a little shorter and perhaps to that extent, better, than the original. But it was not in substance any different from the first version, or from the reformulations that Margaret had derided so fiercely. There was no further comment from that quarter until after I had delivered the Statement. By the time I got back to No. 11 there was a note in her own hand: 'Well done in a difficult

House. We have cut the 5.30 meeting – come this evening [for a pre-arranged working dinner] when you are ready. TV presentation matters more than anything else. Your quiet confidence goes over very well there, as in the House.'

I cannot recall Margaret ever coming closer to an apology than this. Neither of us ever mentioned the incident again.

He describes the Falklands conflict as a time when Margaret Thatcher felt isolated, at least partly because she had no confidence in the strategy of Francis Pym, who had replaced Lord Carrington as Foreign Secretary after his resignation. She would use her regular Sunday evening chats with Geoffrey Howe

> to discuss the 'progress' of Pym's persistent, but intrinsically hopeless, search for an honourable settlement of the Falklands dispute. On those occasions, when I sensed that she felt at her most lonely, we reached perhaps the high point of our relationship. It was clear to me that the Argentine leadership was never seriously committed to such an outcome.
>
> When victory finally came, there was a transformation in Margaret's standing, throughout the world, even more than at home, and deservedly so. There can be no doubting the extraordinary importance, from start to end of the crisis, of her sustained courage in the face of uniquely personalised pressures. The role of victorious warrior queen was one into which she grew very naturally. Her confidence in her own

judgement was certainly not diminished. And her respect for the wisdom of the Foreign Office had certainly not been enhanced by the whole story. Nor, I have to confess, had mine. On the day after the invasion (Saturday 3 April 1982), I had to preside over a ministerial meeting to consider the economic consequences of the conflict. The only department not represented there was the Foreign and Commonwealth Office. 'Surely,' I exploded, 'they're going to send someone along to tell us whether or not there's a war on?' It was a serious question, with important legal consequences, but it went, that day, unanswered. At any rate, these changes in Margaret's perception did not bode well for the years ahead.

Early in their relationship, Geoffrey Howe, like John Wakeham, also devised ways of dealing with what he calls 'the problems of managing Margaret'.

In my case, (at least in my Treasury days) I had the satisfaction of knowing that Margaret and I were working to basically similar guidelines, even if we should not always handle the details in the same way. This sense of ideological security is what came, I suppose, from being 'one of us'. This central sympathy of purpose gave one more rather than less room for manoeuvre in the management of policies. Often indeed I was able to enlarge or accelerate actions on which we both agreed, and less often, to modify or tailor their impact so as to make them more sensitive to the anxieties of others: restraining, for example, Margaret's passionate wish to preserve the real value of mortgage interest relief or even to embark upon the replacement of the rating system.

This kind of unspoken deal is to be found, I suspect, in many management or team relationships – is indeed essential to their survival. It becomes intolerable or unacceptable, either to the partnership itself or to the world that is affected by it, only if the relationship is manifestly or chronically unbalanced or irretrievably fissile.

Margaret's most important weakness – the flipside of her strength – was the extent to which her partners were driven in the end to choose between submission or defection. Perhaps inevitably, the closer the original bonding, the longer the life of the partnership, the more dramatic the final rupture. 'I must prevail' was the phrase that finally broke Nigel Lawson's bond of loyalty and affection. Is almost all real leadership foredoomed to produce such rupture?

In his autobiography, John Major paints a vivid picture of Geoffrey Howe's last Cabinet meeting before his resignation.

His last Cabinet meeting on the morning of his resignation was the worst of all. Geoffrey and Margaret were sitting side by side, directly opposite me. They could hardly bring themselves to look at one another. Geoffrey stared down at his papers, his lips pursed; Margaret had a disdainful air, her eyes glittering. When he looked down the long Cabinet table, she looked up it. When she put her head down to read her notes, he looked straight up. The body language said it all. This treatment of a senior colleague was embarrassing for the whole Cabinet.

That incident took place in the privacy of the Cabinet Room. But Geoffrey Howe's final break with Margaret Thatcher could hardly have been more public. It was televised live from the House of Commons in his resignation speech delivered on 13 November 1990. He concluded his devastating attack with the words, 'the time has come for others to consider their own response to the tragic conflict of loyalties with which I have myself wrestled for perhaps too long'.

For her part, Margaret Thatcher, according to Harvey Thomas's account given above, had an 'unwavering belief that you could say anything and do anything to "trusted friends"'. After Geoffrey Howe's shatteringly dramatic resignation speech, Harvey Thomas remembers having a drink with Mrs Thatcher after a final speech rehearsal. Just before they departed for home, Mrs Thatcher said sadly: 'Why couldn't Geoffrey have just left quietly after these years together as friends?'

As Geoffrey Howe himself put it, on another occasion, 'it didn't always feel like that'.

FOUR

'MAGGIE HAD A HUGE SENSE OF PERSONAL LOYALTY AND PERSONAL RESPONSIBILITY.'

John Major describes Margaret Thatcher as a 'woman of contrasts'. This she certainly was but, he added,

It is worth noting that – however combative she might have been with her peers – she would never once raise her voice to those who were in no position to answer back. This was a Prime Minister who engendered great affection from her staff.

John Wakeham confirms this.

On informal occasions she was always very considerate and kind to her staff. I never came across anyone who did not enjoy working for her and the devotion of many who worked for her years ago is still to this day very much there, and will be there forever.

The accounts written for this book by some of those who worked for and with Margaret Thatcher have produced many examples of her kind and considerate behaviour towards them, often above and beyond mere duty or politeness.

Janice Richards worked in the Prime Minister's Office from 1971 until 1999. She became Head of the Garden Rooms and the Correspondence Section at No. 10 in 1985.

Before I joined No. 10, I worked at the Department of Education and Science in Curzon Street, as it was then named. Mrs Thatcher was the Secretary of State, and, even now, I remember there was a buzz with her at the helm. Little did I know that I would be working for her again in the future, in very different circumstances.

As a Garden Room secretary (so called because the secretaries' rooms overlooked the rear garden at ground level), I, with other colleagues, performed the ritualistic welcoming party for incoming Prime Ministers in the Front Hall of No. 10. May 1979 was the start of a very special welcoming, and we all felt that we were going to experience not only history being made, but different and exciting times ahead. We were proved right, and those memorable years while Mrs Thatcher was in No. 10 proved to be very special times for those privileged to work there.

I was one of twelve secretaries who worked closely with the private office and travelled with the Prime Minister wherever she went, either in the UK or overseas. Especially at Chequers, there was an opportunity to see a more relaxed and less pressured side to Mrs Thatcher. I recall conversations about food, clothes, family and so on.

I recall the visit to Lusaka in 1979, for the Commonwealth heads of government meeting – Mrs Thatcher's first of many – where the heads of state and government were accommodated in Mulungushi, a sort of tribal village complex which Kenneth Kaunda had had specially built some time earlier. However, the bungalows allocated were, to say the least, below standard, and a colleague recalled someone describing them as 'glorified mud huts'. Horizon House was the accommodation for the support staff – far superior to Mrs Thatcher's own, and she joined the staff there after a few days. There were some memorable meals there, all support staff sitting at a large round table with her. Clive Whitmore, at that time Principal Private Secretary to Mrs T., Brian Cartledge, Private Secretary for Overseas Affairs at No. 10, and Sir John Hunt, the Cabinet Secretary, were there too. I also remember that Mrs Thatcher was unwell for a time during the Lusaka visit, but just had to get on with the business of the day. All marvelled at her ability to keep going.

I became Head of the Garden Rooms in 1985 when my travelling days came to an end. This allowed me to work more closely with Mrs Thatcher again, but in a different way. There were decisions to be made on gifts which were to be given, and caretaking the gifts which Mrs Thatcher received. Since she had come to power, the correspondence received had risen to 5,000 letters a week, and one needed to be selective about which should be shown to the private office and the Prime Minister. It was important that she saw a wide range of letters and learned of the personal difficulties and problems experienced by the general public, and thereby the issues that most concerned them. She took a great interest in these letters and would often add manuscript sentences in her responses.

Long-serving staff were permitted to hold their leaving parties in No. 10. Mrs Thatcher's government driver, Ken Godber, was one of these, and I remember at that party that some of those attending could not hear Mrs Thatcher's speech clearly, so she whipped off her shoes and stood on a table!

When her resignation was announced in 1990, No. 10 received many sacks of mail which entailed asking the whole office to help to open. The support she received from the general public was quite overwhelming, and one could see just how touched she was when she sat on the floor with me and my staff, opening and reading just some of those letters. It wasn't only going to be her staff who would miss her.

I feel so very fortunate to have worked at No. 10, and especially while Mrs Thatcher was there. Those who worked with and for Mrs Thatcher felt very privileged, and the admiration and respect they held for her was unquestionable. It was one of those periods when all – political staff, civil servants, protection officers – worked together in the most wonderful family atmosphere in my time in Downing Street, not repeated either before or after Mrs Thatcher's time as Prime Minister.

I was one of those who lined up to welcome Mrs Thatcher in 1979 and again lined up to say farewell in 1990. It was the end of over eleven years of history, eleven happy years, and a sad end to an extraordinary period, her years in Downing Street.

Elizabeth Cottrell, who in Chapter 1 of this book describes working very closely with Margaret Thatcher in the preparation of an important speech, here tells how the evening in question continued. (Elizabeth of course was not a member of Mrs Thatcher's own staff, but on this occasion was working with her in her capacity as Head of Research at the Centre for Policy Studies.)

She takes up the tale of the writing of the speech in the early hours.

Finally Mrs Thatcher decided that we should stop – until the next day. But she must be sure that I was comfortable. So at three o'clock in the morning, the Prime Minister of the United Kingdom was running a bath for me, bringing me a night dress and toothbrush, popping a hot-water bottle into the bed just in case it was cold! Nothing was too much trouble for her – it was incredible.

The cold light of morning did not diminish her kindness. She was at my bedside at 7 a.m. with a cup of tea. At around 8, a maid appeared to cook breakfast. Then it was back to work. When I left at noon, the speech was some 3,500 words long and almost finalised, in good time to be delivered on Monday. The Prime Minister said that she would polish it over the weekend at Chequers.

My extraordinary twenty-four hours was over. I went home, exhausted but elated. The lecture was duly delivered at the Institute of Electrical Engineers on Monday 26 July. Mrs Thatcher's thank-you letter followed promptly. 'It went down rather well, although I say so myself,' she wrote, 'I hope you know how grateful I am.'

I felt that I was the one who should be expressing gratitude for a unique and unforgettable experience.

Margaret Thatcher showed consistent kindness and consideration for Conservative Party workers and volunteers. She had a great and enduring love for the party, took a great interest in its members and staff, and seemed prepared to devote an almost infinite amount of time to it. It could be that her first experience of a Party Conference, in 1946, holds the key to this lifelong enthusiasm for party matters. She had risen up the ranks of the Oxford University Conservative Association to become its President in October 1946. But her passion for the Conservative Party had not won her admirers at her college, Somerville, where the Principal, Dame Janet Vaughan, described her as 'an oddity. Why? She was a Conservative. She stood out. Somerville had always been a radical establishment and there weren't many Conservatives about. We used to argue about politics. She was so set in steel as a Conservative' (Campbell, *Margaret Thatcher*, p.50). But when the young Margaret Roberts arrived at the Party Conference held in Blackpool that year, 1946, she was 'immediately entranced. So often in Grantham and in Oxford it had felt unusual to be a Conservative. Now suddenly I was with hundreds of other people who believed as I did and who shared my insatiable appetite for talking politics' (Thatcher, *The Path to Power*). After the icy intellectual, political and probably social condescension proffered by Oxford, it must have seemed heady indeed.

From observation, I believe that she was unique among her predecessors and successors as Prime Minister (with the probable exception of John Major) in that she positively loved contact with supporters, and nowhere more than at the Conference. Many's the minister I have heard complaining about 'having to do the Conference', or 'having to do a party rally'. I have always wondered why. Do they not realise that politics is about people and support? Margaret Thatcher never doubted it, nor the fact that it was a two-way process.

Like Janice Richards, Harvey Thomas was also at a Commonwealth heads of government meeting in 1985.

Maggie had a huge sense of personal loyalty and personal responsibility. After the meeting in Lusaka, I had travelled ahead to New York to prepare for her speech at the fortieth anniversary of the United Nations. In those days, Prime Ministers were away from their countries for longer than they ever are today and she had been out of the country for close to two weeks when she came to the hotel in New York.

While she had been away, a Cabinet member had been having a quiet go at me and my style of presentation, largely through the Peterborough column in the Daily Telegraph. *Nothing too serious, but enough to hurt a bit, as these things do when you read them about yourself.*

I never found out how she picked up on it after being out of the country for two weeks, but she strode into the hotel room where I was waiting and her first words were, 'Hello, Harvey dear, I hear they've been saying silly things about you in the Peterborough column. Don't worry, dear, I know where it's coming from and it will stop as soon as I get back to London.' And it did!

She had a huge capacity to focus both on individual issues and her overarching objective of 'making Britain great again'. Because this was such a passion for her, it took precedence, not over family and loved ones, but over all the routine activities that are part of daily life.

Having spent fifteen years working for Dr Billy Graham, I had already learned the importance of 'the right time'. Hundreds of people, during the thirteen-and-a-half years I worked for Mrs Thatcher, asked me if I would introduce them to her, and there were probably not more than a dozen occasions in all that time when I felt it appropriate to do so.

On one occasion, my parents-in-law, Erich and Irene, were visiting Marlies and me in London. I had no thoughts of introducing them, but in the constituency office one afternoon, the 'timing' was suddenly exactly right. Mrs T. asked how they were, and it was just the right time for me to ask if I could bring them into the office the next day to meet her, and of course she was delighted, and we have wonderful photographs.

Doreen Miller, who in 1982 was a candidate in the European elections, recalls

the usual photo call for candidates to be photographed with the Prime Minister. She came to the meeting, but announced that as she had a very bad cold she preferred not to have the photographs taken. I remarked to my neighbour, quietly as I thought, 'What a shame, I wanted to give a copy to my ailing father for his birthday.' She obviously heard me, because she immediately said that if I wanted a picture for my father she would do it, despite not feeling or looking at her best.

There was a similar act of kindness, also indirectly involving my father, who died in April 1986. My brother was in London for the funeral, and, while he was there, I took him to an Association afternoon tea, which Mrs Thatcher was attending. She immediately sought us out, having heard of our loss, and despite there being many other guests to meet, took the time to spend a few minutes with us both, asking about my father and offering us both very sincere condolences.

Joan Seccombe remembers Mrs Thatcher, with Denis, her election team and the famous battle bus, visiting her house before an election rally in Solihull during the 1987 election campaign. They filled the house and the lane leading to it for about two hours, while

Margaret perfected her speech and Denis watched the Test match on television with my husband. The battle bus was huge and took up the entire lane, stopping any traffic from our neighbours' getting past. This would not normally have caused any problems, but, unknown to me, it coincided with a young family moving in next door and meant that the removal people could not leave for the duration of the visit. Far from becoming angry and impatient, our new neighbours lined the lane as the bus moved on, cheering and waving excitedly as she left. The next day, I received a handwritten thank-you letter – this was true of wherever she visited and the letters always showed such warm appreciation with a personal touch. This was shown again when my husband had a stroke while we were away in Switzerland. Somehow, Margaret found time to send a two-page handwritten letter wishing us well, and offering generous support. I shall always treasure it. These personal touches are at odds with the public image of the Iron Lady, and extraordinary and brilliant as Margaret's political career was, I consider myself incredibly fortunate to have been able to see this side of her as well.

David Simpson at the time of the 1983 general election was a deputy Central Office agent working in the Greater London area and based in Conservative Central Office at 32 Smith Square.

Now we all know that the Prime Minister was a strong lady, but within that external strength there was also an inner kindness and so it was that at the Greater London election rally held at the Wembley Arena on Sunday 5 June 1983, that inner kindness shone through.

This was the final major Conservative rally of the campaign, orchestrated by Harvey Thomas, the larger-than-life Head of Communications at Central Office. The Wembley Arena was packed, the legendary DJ and comedian Kenny Everett was the warm-up act, and he also introduced a number of other celebrities from the world of sport and show business. What a show he gave, and with Cecil Parkinson, the Party Chairman, with his urbane charm, the scene was set for a rousing campaign speech.

The Prime Minister came on to a rapturous reception, it seemed to matter not a jot what she said because everyone knew she was going to win and they all wanted to be part of that victory, and to be able to say, 'I was there!'

Once the rally was over, and those of us who had been responsible for the stewarding could relax, I adjourned to the green room with my family. It was there, over tea and biscuits, that Mrs Thatcher saw my nine-year-old daughter and seven-year-old son, both with their autograph books and clearly wanting to approach her. They didn't have to wait long. Autographs were given, followed by an animated chat, at the end of which the Prime Minister said she thought it was a

great pity they were not yet of voting age as they had both shown real
interest in her politics. They were thrilled, and were able the next day
to tell the story to teachers and school friends alike.

One of the most enduring myths about Margaret Thatcher
is that she loathed and detested the civil service and civil
servants. It is true that she was impatient with some of the
machinery of Whitehall, which she regarded as impeding
the progress of government policy. But it is also true that
many civil servants appreciated her ability to master a
detailed brief, and her efforts to understand exactly what
went on in government departments.

Ian Beesley, who served in the Rayner/Efficiency Unit
from 1981 to 1986, writes,

It was during that first assignment that I realised that though Mrs
Thatcher disliked the civil service, she appreciated individual civil
servants and especially those with a bias towards action whom she
perceived were trying to change things for the better. Breaking with
tradition, two of the early scrutiny examining officers in the Unit,
Norman Warner of the DHSS and Clive Ponting of the MoD, were
summoned to present their findings in person; and during 1980 she
told Rayner that she wanted a Downing Street reception to thank the
'Rayner supporters' for their efforts. Spouses were to be invited too,
because they also played a vital part in supporting their husbands/
wives. Much consternation followed. What about those who had
partners but were unmarried? What would this forbidding woman
think if they were to be invited? Well, eventually someone plucked up

the courage and asked. What is all the fuss about was the answer, of course partners were to be invited, formal status had nothing to do with it. This awareness of the contribution made by the families of those who worked in the civil or diplomatic service was a recurrent concern.

The reception was on 3 December in Downing Street. A vivid memory is of the Prime Minister kicking off her shoes, climbing on the grand piano and giving an impromptu speech of thanks to her young reformers while Michael Alison (her PPS) tugged at the skirts of her evening gown because she was keeping an appointment waiting in the House of Commons.

At a personal level she treated us with courtesy and respect. We were neither invisible servants nor privileged. You were only as good as your last intervention and you had better keep at the forefront of your mind that government spent other people's hard-earned money. Rayner's maxim, 'treat every pound as if it were your own', might well have come from her. But when my successor was involved in a bad car accident, her concern was open and genuine.

Nothing could be further from the caricature of a Prime Minister/Cabinet Secretary relationship depicted in the TV series *Yes, Minister,* than the one between Margaret Thatcher and Robert Armstrong, Secretary of the Cabinet from 1979 to 1987.

He gives an example.

As regards Spycatcher, when it became clear that a witness would be required to attend the court in New South Wales to speak to the affidavit entered by the British government in support of its application for an injunction to prevent the publication of Peter Wright's book, I discussed with the Prime Minister and others who should be sent. The conclusion reached was that I should be chosen for this task. The Prime Minister did not instruct me to go; she asked whether I was prepared to go. Since I agreed with the conclusion, I said that I was. While I was out there, she spoke to me on the telephone two or three times to ask how I was bearing up. When I came home, she gave me a couple of bottles of whisky as an expression of her appreciation.

In my last few hours of service, on New Year's Eve 1987, my wife and I entertained the Prime Minister and Denis Thatcher at a perfor-mance of Die Fledermaus *at the Royal Opera House. After the performance, we went back to Downing Street and saw the New Year in with a glass of champagne. It was a happy way to celebrate and give thanks for a crowded and happy eight years of working with Mrs Thatcher and for a close and rewarding relationship of trust and friendship.*

According to the myth that Margaret Thatcher loathed all civil servants, and the Foreign Office even more, Sir Richard Parsons should have suffered a double disadvan-tage in her eyes, as an ambassador. It was not the case.

The last time I saw her was when I went back to England for the formal launching of a splendid new ferry to operate between the English coast and Gothenburg in western Sweden. The Swedish owner of the shipping line had invited me to accompany him in his private plane. The ceremony was to be performed by the British Prime Minister, but I did not comment on that to my Swedish hosts. It is usually a mistake to boast that you personally know important people, because there is always the danger that they will fail to recognise you and that will make you look a fool.

Not on this occasion. As soon as Mrs T. appeared, regally dressed, she shouted out with enthusiasm, 'Hello, Richard, how nice to see you again.' The Swedes were duly impressed, not least by my modesty in failing to reveal that I rubbed shoulders with the great and the good.

Interestingly, when I was posted from Madrid to Stockholm in 1984 I heard that Mrs T. had sent her Private Secretary to the FCO to ask, in vain, whether I could not be given a more demanding final post.

Even parliamentary colleagues with reservations about Margaret Thatcher's policies were impressed by her acts of spontaneous kindness. Patrick Cormack is one of these.

At the time of the Poulson scandal,† a number of Members came in for severe criticism in a rather damning report. One of these was John Cordle, the Member for Bournemouth East. A group of us met with him on the Thursday before the report was due to be debated on the following Monday. We told him that there really was a chance that the House would expel him and that it would be far better if he were to seize the high ground and resign, by applying for the Chiltern Hundreds and making a statement in the House before doing so. Convinced of his own innocence, very probably rightly, but conscious of the witch-hunt atmosphere that was developing, he reluctantly took

---

† A major political corruption scandal sparked by the discovery that architectural designer and businessman John Poulson had engaged in widespread bribery of politicians, civil servants and local authority officials. The Select Committee inquiry reported in 1977.

this advice and on the Friday morning made his statement. The late Sir Peter Mills, Member for Devon West, and I sat on either side of him as he did so. Peter then had to dash back to his constituency and so I had the task of looking after John Cordle and taking him to the Chief Whip's office. We were joined there by Margaret, who had sat on the front bench with him, talking to him and even holding his hand. There was nothing synthetic about this. This was genuine human warmth and real kindness.

And that remained part of her makeup, even throughout her premiership. In 1982, my then agent, a young man of twenty-five, had one of the very first heart transplants in the country. Initially, it was a great success (sadly, he died a couple of years later), and I took him, apparently miraculously restored, to the Party Conference in Brighton, where on the eve of her Conference speech, Margaret Thatcher devoted a couple of hours to seeing Andrew in her room, feeding him cake and biscuits, and talking fondly, knowledgeably and sympathetically, as if she had been a combination of family doctor and favourite aunt. It was truly remarkable to witness.

Michael Jopling, as Chief Whip, was able to observe what he describes as her

caring and understanding nature. Before her first Christmas as Prime Minister, she asked me if I knew of any of our MPs who were going to be alone over that time, as she wanted to invite them to Chequers. Again, when people both in or out of Parliament got into trouble over various sexual misdemeanours, she would comment that her experience as a barrister had taught her that 'some men cannot resist feasting with leopards'.

John MacGregor recalls an informal lunch at Chequers when Mrs Thatcher had 'an urgent and rather complicated matter' that she wanted to discuss with him.

We arranged that we should arrive early so that she could do so. As we arrived at the security gates half an hour earlier than the others for this purpose, Jean, my wife, wondered what she should do while she was on her own before the rest of the guests arrived. She need not have worried. As we drove into the courtyard, Margaret was waiting at the front door. She greeted Jean effusively, took her in, showed her round and arranged for her to be properly looked after, and only then came down to our meeting.

Jill Knight was elected as MP for Edgbaston in 1966 seven years after Mrs Thatcher.

I also fought twice in a hopeless seat before I managed it. When I arrived in the House of Commons, to my surprise, she knew my history and welcomed me warmly. She referred to a speech I had made years earlier at a Conservative Conference, which actually achieved a standing ovation. That she should recall it at all amazed me. But she also offered to help and advise whenever I thought I needed it, and very generously was as good as her word when I did.

Virginia Bottomley fought the Isle of Wight seat in 1983.

Arriving in the Isle of Wight by hovercraft, Margaret Thatcher came to support my first parliamentary campaign on the penultimate day of the 1983 general election. She was magnificent. 'It was as though she was re-taking the Falkland Islands,' said the sketchwriters. Her charisma, authority and confidence had started the transformation of Britain's economy, regained the Falkland Islands and established her in Downing Street. I may have made a reputation as a serious campaigner with over 34,000 votes; I failed to win the seat.

Rebuilding her Cabinet, having successfully gained a second term, on the day after the election and my failure to win, the telephone rang. The Prime Minister was on the line. She was empathetic, generous, delightful. This reduced me to tears. It was a typical example of her personal kindness to individuals and the ability to offer support to someone of relative insignificance, even though she had a fearsome diary and heavy responsibilities.

And even John Monks, in no way as he puts it 'a paid-up member of the Mrs Thatcher fan club', noted with approval a vignette at a No. 10 reception:

I was at a reception at No. 10 including a collection of the great and the good, with Jacqueline du Pré, then badly afflicted by multiple sclerosis and in a wheelchair. Mrs Thatcher entered and went straight over to the great cellist, a favourite of mine, and they talked intently for twenty minutes or so. It is not easy to talk to anyone for more than a minute at a crowded reception, yet she ignored all others and applied her concentration, an act of personal kindness which sticks in my mind.

A woman of contrasts indeed.

FIVE

'I HOPE THAT ONE QUALITY IN WHICH I AM NOT LACKING IS COURAGE.'

Few of Margaret Thatcher's critics could advance the argument that she lacked courage. The challenges that she faced and overcame during her premiership demonstrated again and again her steely resolve.

For Michel Jopling, her Chief Whip until 1983, the three greatest tests were the Falklands War, the Brighton bomb and the Miners' Strike.

> *In all of these challenges there was a common theme. There must be no question of giving way. The challenge must be met and overcome. The rule of law and the right of the government to govern must be asserted. I remember her calmness which was so apparent in meeting all these challenges.*

But before there was any thought of her becoming an

MP, let alone Prime Minister, she faced down unpopularity and, worse, condescension and ridicule at Oxford for her unfashionable Conservative views. She also, like other women, endured extraordinary prejudice from mostly male selection committees before she got a parliamentary seat.

Jill Knight shared the problem. She entered Parliament in 1966, seven years after Margaret Thatcher.

Today, if one has ambitions to become an MP, it is a positive advantage to be a woman. Fifty years ago, it was a monumental disadvantage. Selection committees did not like females. Very few women even had their names put forward for consideration, much less for an interview. It was difficult to build up a reputation for political knowledge, let alone expertise, and the general feeling was that the electorate would not vote for a woman, so why choose one to be a candidate? Only ample amounts of dedication, courage, intelligence, hard work, persistence and personality broke the barriers, and Margaret Thatcher had every one of them. She was young and pretty, too, which may have helped. Contesting the strong Labour seat of Dartford in 1950 did not get her into Parliament, but it brought her more publicity, more fans and much valuable experience. She fought it again in 1951, still without success, but her determination, loyalty and courage, added to the ability which by now everyone recognised, finally got her the nomination for the plum seat of Finchley and she became its Member in 1959.

That, of course, was only part of the story. In 1954, when the Thatchers were living in Orpington, Margaret Thatcher tried for the seat when the sitting MP, Sir

Waldron Smithers, died at the end of that year. She was shortlisted, but the Association chose its own chairman, Donald Sumner, as the candidate. Ironically, when Sumner resigned the seat seven years later to become a judge, it was sensationally lost in the famous Orpington by-election to the Liberal candidate, Eric Lubbock, an outcome unthinkable had the Orpington Tories chosen Margaret Thatcher as their candidate in the first place.

In 1956, she put her name back on the Central Office candidates list, and took part in a course in television skills for hopeful candidates. The following year, when her children were three years old, she resumed her search for a winnable seat. Beckenham came up in early 1957. She was up against three men candidates and one of them, Philip Goodhart, was selected. Apparently some of the Beckenham Conservative Association members had specified that they wanted someone local, preferably a businessman or one with parliamentary experience. Such mantras are very familiar to all would-be candidates. Associations usually add that their particular seat is extremely safe and should be awarded only to a very deserving candidate.

Towards the end of 1957, Lady Davidson indicated that she was standing down from her Hemel Hempstead seat. Margaret Thatcher at once said that she was interested, but a shortlist of six men was drawn up. None impressed the selection committee, so a second list was compiled, this time including Margaret Thatcher, who was rejected with the comment 'limited outlook'. She then applied and was shortlisted for Maidstone, where she was beaten by John Wells.

Finally, Finchley came up; Margaret Thatcher applied and was selected, despite the fact that the deputy area agent (a woman) reported: 'I gather that Finchley are determined to see some women so that they may be seen to have gone through the motions, but I should be very surprised if they selected one.'

Like so many women candidates in all the main political parties, Margaret Thatcher must have raged against what she very well knew was prejudice against her because she was a woman. It took real grit for her to continue against what must have seemed insuperable odds. Even in Finchley, at her final adoption meeting (the formal meeting by which an Association officially adopts the successful applicant as their candidate), there were a few dissenting voices.

When I was selected for my seat in South West Norfolk in 1986, the local Association members had determined from the start that there were two kinds of candidate they did not want and would not have: 'a barrister from away, or a woman'. In the event, they began by choosing a barrister from away, an able lawyer called Charles Harris, whereupon a grassroots rebellion was organised to reject him at his actual adoption meeting, normally a formality. The whole process was started again, and on the second attempt, they chose me, the other thing they did not want, a woman. And at my adoption meeting, three members resigned publicly, saying as they left the room that they could not go home and say to people in their villages that the next MP would be a woman.

I include my own selection story because, like scores of other women candidates (and men, although they were not normally rejected because they were men), I know it is tough to go on and on with the process of getting a seat after a number of rejections. You have to keep going, but you steel yourself every time for yet another failure. My story is far from the worst in my generation. Emily Blatch, who eventually became Deputy Leader of the House of Lords, after a successful ministerial career at the Home Office and Education, was asked at a selection meeting if she realised that the House of Commons was in London and that she would have to go there if she became an MP. Ann Widdecombe was asked if she did not think she was rather short to be an MP. Judith Chaplin, the tragically short-lived MP for Newbury from 1992, was introduced at a selection meeting in Surrey with the words, 'This is Judith Chaplin. She is from Norfolk where she and her second husband have nine children between them.' She was then ushered to a podium which was so high that it obscured her from the view of the audience.

We all knew that we had to keep going. The fact that Margaret Thatcher had gone before was a comfort to all of us.

Understandably (although this did not accord with the popular image of her), she was very vulnerable

where family matters were concerned. When her son
Mark was reported missing during a motor rally in the
Sahara in January 1982, she had six days of appalling
anxiety, and was frequently found weeping, sometimes
in public. It did not stop her doing her job, as John
MacGregor observed.

*One of my ministerial appointments in the early 1980s was
Parliamentary Under-Secretary for the Department of Trade and
Industry, with special responsibilities for small businesses. I was
generally known as the Minister for Small Businesses, or, indeed, as
the Small Business Minister. It was a time when we were trying to
reinstate the importance of small businesses, to revive the spirit of
enterprise and to assist the growth of start-ups. Early on, I arranged
a one-day conference for small businesses, their federations and organisations at the Russell Hotel in London. The highlight was to be an
address by Margaret Thatcher at lunchtime. Mid-morning, I heard
the news that Mark, Margaret's son, had been lost in the Sahara
Desert. I assumed that she would cancel. But no, word came that
she was determined to go ahead, I am sure because of the importance
that she attached to these policies, given her own family background
and her huge personal commitment to the sector. As she got out of
the car, she was uncharacteristically tearful and it was clear that
she was very upset. I waited in the room with her for ten minutes
while she tried to get further news. Then she turned to me and said,
'Right, John', stood up very composed, went straight into the lunch
and delivered a marvellous speech. No one there could have known the
inner turmoil.*

The Falklands conflict certainly stretched her to the very limit. She was acutely aware that the final decision to send Britain to war was hers, and she had to take responsibility for it. What turned out, in the end, to be a great political triumph for Margaret Thatcher began with a failure of foreign policy, in that her government had apparently been unable to decide between cutting defence spending and maintaining overseas defence commitments.

From the start of the affair, she realised that she had to pay punctilious attention to Cabinet and parliamentary procedures in a matter as serious as going to war. She had to seek and get the approval of the Cabinet and Parliament. She would have unquestionably have resigned had the Cabinet not agreed. Parliament also gave its approval, albeit on a technical motion on the day, but, she wrote in her memoirs, 'I obtained the almost unanimous but grudging support of a Commons that was anxious to support the government's policy, while reserving judgement on the government's performance.' She set up a small War Cabinet, technically an offshoot of the standing Cabinet Committee for Overseas and Defence, known as OD(SA). This War Cabinet met once and sometimes twice a day throughout the war, and a second full Cabinet meeting met each week after the War Cabinet, so that it was fully informed at every stage. The Chiefs of Staff were present at this second full Cabinet.

Peter Hennessy quotes a Whitehall insider in *The Prime Minister*:

They were proper Cabinets with proper decisions. She was aware that the nearer she got, the surer she had to be that people were with her ... She was seen as an able and acceptable leader of a team of people ... She spent much more time asking questions and weighing up the answers than she is reputed to have done in all other areas. With hindsight, the fact that she was a woman, that she did not have military experience and that she had a clear and penetrating mind were all pluses.

Ian Beesley describes how the decision to sink the *Belgrano* was taken at an emergency meeting of OD(SA) at Chequers on 2 May 1982.

Uncharacteristically, Margaret Thatcher did not lead with her opinion. She asked each person in turn, ministers and officials, whether an order to sink the Belgrano *should be given, before she gave any hint of her own position.*

The fact was that the only person whose career would have been irretrievably destroyed by failure in the Falklands conflict was Margaret Thatcher. She was acutely aware of this throughout. When others had prevaricated, she had acted. And, in the end, she took immense personal pleasure and pride from the outcome. Most agree that her whole leadership style changed as a result.

But the conflict took a personal toll on Margaret Thatcher. At the time of the Falklands conflict, Joan

Seccombe was the Chairman of the Conservative Women's National Committee.

During the Falklands conflict she showed typically amazing courage. I had seen her before her session began at the Conservative Women's Annual Conference in spring 1982. Her concern over the injuries to our troops and their families nearly overwhelmed her as, that morning, the Atlantic Conveyor *was hit, killing twelve sailors and injuring many, many more. When she arrived at the conference, her officials were unsure of the number of casualties and she was clearly distressed. It was made clear to her that the world's media would be focused on her at this crucial point. As ever, she showed courage and impeccable judgement. She went out on the stage, and delivered a speech with strength and determination, while at the same time sharing the grief with the families of the young people who had lost their lives or were injured during the conflict. This test of character was one which she passed with flying colours and I felt people were able to draw comfort from her courage and fortitude throughout this difficult time.*

Harvey Thomas, who as Head of Presentation at Conservative Central Office was in charge of the conference, throws further light on the Prime Minister's reaction – and how it was handled.

Her personal acceptance of responsibility was both straightforward and sometimes painful for friends to see.

The day a British warship was hit in the Falklands, there was a Conservative Women's conference scheduled in the Royal Horticultural

Hall. Backstage, Margaret's tears flowed for almost forty minutes as she felt the burden of being, as she put it, 'the first Prime Minister in decades to have to send young British soldiers to their death in conflict'.

We had many extra speakers at that conference, and so I bundled them up to the platform to keep it going while she composed herself.

There was much media comment during and after the Falklands War, alleging that Margaret Thatcher had shown little feeling for the casualties suffered on both sides as a result of the conflict, and that she had somehow gloried in going to war. The fact is that she took the whole matter with the utmost seriousness, paid the greatest possible attention to the democratic process throughout, and was deeply grieved by the loss of life and her responsibility for it. That same sense of personal responsibility coloured her reaction to the bombing by the IRA of the Grand Hotel in Brighton when the Conservative Party Conference was taking place there on 12 October 1984. Four people were killed outright by the bomb, one died a month later and thirty-four were taken to hospital with their injuries. Harvey Thomas recalls that Margaret Thatcher

believed that people were hurt, as she saw it, because the IRA was trying to kill her. In a personal handwritten note the following week, she said, 'It would have been difficult to have gone through last weekend without a strong faith.' Years later she spoke again of 'the burden of responsibility' when speaking about the Tebbits, who had been so terribly injured in the incident.

Three of the contributors to this book have written accounts of the Brighton bomb. I have included all three in full because, while the accounts overlap, they complement one another in their vivid depiction of the terrifying attack.

Joan Seccombe had become Vice-Chairman of the National Union (the voluntary side of the Conservative Party) by 1984.

The 1984 Conservative Party Conference in Brighton was one which changed many lives, due to the extraordinary events which unfolded. On the Thursday evening, 11 October, we had retired to bed in Room 19 on the third floor of the Grand Hotel when there was the most enormous explosion followed by a strange rumbling sound, which we later found out was the building collapsing in on itself. Lights went out, bells rang furiously. We dressed, partially, with speed and left by the emergency exit fire escape. The main staircase was blocked so our route was through Lady Airey's room. I will always remember emerging from the Grand Hotel and seeing Sir Keith Joseph standing immaculately on the seafront, resplendent and bedecked in cravat and silk dressing gown! We went into the adjoining Metropole Hotel, and were generously provided with refreshments throughout the night. Nobody quite knew what had happened to others staying in the hotel, but we were assured that the Prime Minister was safe and had been whisked away.

Seven people lost their lives and some were horribly injured, particularly Norman and Margaret Tebbit, who still bear the scars today. We had no idea what would happen next, but Margaret, as ever, led from the front. At 9.30 a.m., the scheduled time for the conference to begin, she was on show, immaculately dressed and with an air of calm about her. Her actions steadied the atmosphere for the nation and the session proceeded as organised, even if the dress of the day was not always as planned. In the afternoon, with a speech hastily amended, she showed her true sense of leadership, her defiance of terrorism and her determination to have business as usual. After the conference, and with practically no sleep, she went to the Brighton Hospital where she spent many hours with those who had been injured. I found it immensely inspiring and comforting to have a Prime Minister with such strength, courage and compassion.

Sir Anthony Garner was one of the most senior Central Office officials at the Conference that year.

I had a remarkable escape. During the summer my wife and I had gone to the Conservative Women's Ball with friends. One won the lucky programme prize – a week for two at Champneys – and she kindly invited my wife to join her. I suggested that they went during the Party Conference when I would be away from home. Because of this, instead of having a double room at the front of the hotel I had a single room, two rooms away from where I would normally have been.

At 2 a.m. I went up in the lift with Eric Taylor, the North West Area Chairman and a dear friend of mine. We said goodnight on the third floor and he went on up to his room. That was the last I saw of him. When the bomb went off, his room and others, one of which I would have occupied, collapsed, and the occupants fell to the basement. He died there a few hours later. The Prime Minister and Denis, in their room near the centre of the explosion, also had a remarkable escape. It must have been a terrifying experience for them both and they were lucky to live through it. They were quickly taken by the police to a 'safe house' where they remained for the rest of the night.

At about 5 a.m., I went with John Gummer, the Party Chairman, to a meeting with the Chief Constable at Police HQ. We discussed whether or not the final session of the conference should continue that morning. The police said that although a full search of the hall was being conducted, they could not guarantee that there was no further device. We ourselves had to consider whether or not sufficient members would, in the circumstances, attend. Both the chairman and I felt that we should continue if at all possible. John phoned Mrs Thatcher at the 'safe house'. The conversation went something like this. 'Margaret, we are here with the Chief Constable discussing whether or not we should continue with the conference in the morning.' Immediately, she replied, 'Yes, and we must start promptly at 9.30 a.m. I myself will be there at 9.15.' There was no further comment on either side.

We were not allowed back into the hotel and that morning I was still dressed in my very dusty dinner jacket and a tie I had borrowed from one of our stalls at the conference. When Mrs T. arrived at the hall promptly at 9.15 a.m., I took her into a small room at the back of the stage. I assured her that there was a full house and that everyone was very cheerful and looking forward to her speech. She was delighted. While I was talking to her, I was sitting on a table opposite to her. Suddenly she said, 'Tony, do you realise that you have odd shoes on?' In the darkness of my room I had picked up one black brogue and one Oxford shoe! That seemed to me a real example of her attention to detail. She was a remarkable woman who, despite her

terrible experience, remained extremely cool and gave a great speech at
the final session of the conference.

Tom King was also at Brighton for the Party Conference.

One particular memory of working with Margaret Thatcher was her
courage and fortitude in dangerous times. There was no question that
during that active period of IRA terrorism she was their prime target,
and yet she faced it with great courage and resolution at all times.

None of us who were in the Grand Hotel that night will ever forget
the shock of that bomb attack, even though, thankfully, the robustness
of the hotel prevented a far greater loss of life than would otherwise
have been the case. The bomb went off at around 3 a.m. There was at
the time great uncertainty as to whether that would be the only bomb
or whether, a favourite tactic of the IRA, there would be a follow-up
with a further ambush or other attack. Margaret Thatcher was fortu-
nately uninjured even though her room was damaged. However, she
was able to move and it was decided she should go immediately via the
Brighton police station to Lewes. She can hardly have had two hours'
sleep before she awoke to hear of the sad deaths, including Roberta
Wakeham and Tony Berry, and the injuries to John Wakeham and to
Norman and Margaret Tebbit.

She immediately determined that the conference would go on and of
course it was the final day, at which she was due to give the concluding
speech. I shall never forget the reception that the whole hall gave at
9.30 that morning, when Margaret Thatcher and the Cabinet and
the National Union Officers marched on to the platform, on time,
for the opening of the conference. Nor will I forget the courage of the

speech that she then delivered, making clear that democracy would not be defeated by terrorism, that our conference was not going to be disrupted, and that that message of resolution stood out so clearly on that day.

I was not an MP at the time of the Brighton bomb attack, but the enormity of the outrage, a terrorist attack designed to wipe out the whole of the democratically elected government of the country, took some time to sink in, at least partly because of the immediate horror of the deaths and injuries, and the inevitable appalled speculation of what might have been. Margaret Thatcher's demeanour, outwardly totally calm, in control and resolute, hid the fear she must have been feeling, indeed was feeling according to Hugo Young.

Privately she was as terrified, according to friends, as any human being would expect to be. How could anyone shake off the knowledge that she, she in particular, and above all was the target? The event moved her far more deeply than her somewhat routine public expressions of bravado might have indicated.

Three years later, she was required to summon up further reserves of courage on the occasion of the IRA atrocity on Remembrance Day at Enniskillen. Tom King, by that time Secretary of State for Northern Ireland, describes what happened.

I remembered Brighton so well again three years later, November 1987, when the IRA detonated a bomb at the Remembrance Day Parade in Enniskillen. I got to Enniskillen that afternoon, and saw the terrible destruction and loss of life that that outrage had caused. I expressed my conviction at the time that such outrages would not deter the people of Northern Ireland from their determination to live their lives in the future in peace and not be dictated to by terrorism. This was echoed quite soon afterwards by a statement from the British Legion, saying that they were not going to allow their parade to be prevented in this way, and that they would hold another parade two weeks later. This was widely supported across the whole of the United Kingdom by other Legion branches who were determined to send their support. A huge number of standard bearers proposed to attend the re-enactment of the Remembrance Day parade in the square at Enniskillen. As Secretary of State for Northern Ireland, I certainly wished to attend the parade, but I then realised that it would be even better if Margaret Thatcher, as Prime Minister of the United Kingdom, was able to attend as well. I discussed it with Charles Powell, her Private Secretary, and asked if it would be possible for her to come to Enniskillen, and what engagements she had on that day. It then turned out that she had committed to a meeting with President Mitterand in Paris. I asked what time that meeting was, and it turned out that she was due to be there in the afternoon. That meant, with the help of the RAF, that it would be possible for her to come to Enniskillen in the morning, by flying direct to Aldergrove, travel by helicopter to St Angelo base close to Enniskillen and to drive in to the parade. When this was put to her, there wasn't a moment's hesitation and she agreed, indeed, wished, to attend.

Of course the fact of her being committed to go to France for her meeting with President Mitterand was the perfect cover when some press queries arose in the two weeks before the next parade, as to whether she might be attending, when we could say she was going to France. There is no doubt that the security did work and I shall never forget, as we got out of the car in the square in Enniskillen, the collective gasp of recognition from the huge crowd as she stepped out and took her place in the line beside the war memorial.

Her action in attending the parade had a huge impact right across Northern Ireland. There had been great distress at the outrage, particularly among the Unionist community, that it should have occurred on Remembrance Day, such an important day for so many in the Province. That act of leadership by her in being present, and showing her resolution and support for the Province, showed great courage and had a particularly valuable impact on attitudes in the Province. The parade itself was given blanket coverage on television throughout the morning by BBC and ITV, and further enhanced the virtually universal condemnation of the outrage from both Unionist and Nationalist communities, and was a major setback for the IRA and Sinn Féin. There is no question that Margaret Thatcher's presence gave a real focus to the coming together of the whole community, and strong leadership just when it was needed.

Sometimes that courage was misplaced, certainly in the view of party colleagues and the press. This was the position when she was required to reply to an emergency Commons debate called by Labour on the Westland affair on 27 January 1986. Briefly, the Westland affair started in 1985 with a dispute between Leon Brittan at the Department of Trade and Industry and Michael Heseltine at the Ministry of Defence, about a possible rescue package for Westland Helicopters based in Somerset. Leon Brittan favoured a merger with the US helicopter giant Sikorsky; Heseltine, a European consortium of helicopter manufacturers. This escalated into a full-blown row, with accusations of unconstitutional behaviour on the part of Margaret Thatcher, leaks, secret press briefings, all of which culminated in Michael Heseltine's dramatic resignation from the Cabinet. I will not rehearse the rights and wrongs of the convoluted issue here. Suffice it to say that the role of the government, Margaret Thatcher's government, in the matter seemed not entirely above suspicion. The debate, as the opposition well knew, would provide a dramatic parliamentary opportunity to expose that role once and for all. The Prime Minister said on a number of occasions that as she left Downing Street for the debate, she did not know if she would be Prime Minister when she returned. As is frequently the case, what was billed as a knockout parliamentary occasion failed to live up to expectations, not least because Neil Kinnock as opposition leader simply did not manage to deliver a killer blow. Margaret Thatcher herself admitted having made mistakes: 'With hindsight, it is clear that this was one, and doubtless there were others, of a number of matters which could have been handled better, and that too, I regret.'

But the occasion left her washed out and exhausted.

Peter Riddell, at that time Political Editor of the *Financial Times*, paints a haunting picture of the Prime Minister.

> *Only once did I see the mask fall, in January 1986, after the end of the great Westland debate in the House of Commons. After weeks of infighting, disclosures, and resignation of two Cabinet ministers, her hold on power appeared to be under threat. The case against her and her advisers in Downing Street was strong. That morning, as she left for the Commons, she said that might be her last day as Prime Minister. In the event, Neil Kinnock made a mess of his attack on her, she delivered a competent reply, and Michael Heseltine, her great challenger, drew a line under the affair in what Michael Foot called his re-ratting speech. And despite everything, the Tory Party did not want all the upheaval and divisions of changing their leader. When the dramas of the afternoon had been played out, I bumped into her with Archie Hamilton, her faithful PPS, in one of the small corridors by the terrace. I made some no doubt inane remark about the debate and she replied, for once incoherently, looking utterly drained and exhausted. The curtain had fallen, the exam was over, the final lap had been run, and the victor had nothing left.*

Any minister who has faced a hostile House of Commons, with no way of knowing how the day will end, will recognise the courage with which Margaret Thatcher faced her destiny in that fateful debate.

The final word is given to Douglas Hurd, who records Margaret Thatcher's heroic stoicism at the end of her prime ministerial career.

I have a vivid memory of Margaret Thatcher at President Mitterand's banquet at Versailles after the signing of the CSCE Treaty [Conference on Security and Cooperation in Europe Treaty] in the last week of her premiership. She carried herself magnificently that evening, even though she had in her handbag the results of the first ballot in which she failed to achieve a knockout blow against Michael Heseltine.

She must have known it was the beginning of the end. Not for a moment did her demeanour betray that to those watching her on the international stage. That is courage.

SIX

'ONCE YOU HAVE BEEN A CANDIDATE, EVERYTHING ELSE PALLS.'

To read the comments of people who knew her at Oxford, one would never have thought that Margaret Roberts would have become the dazzling premier who fascinated the British press, an American, a French and a Russian President, and whose sobriquet, the Iron Lady, became known across the world.

Pamela Mason, a contemporary of Margaret Thatcher's at Somerville, remembers 'a plump bonny girl, quite well covered. She had brown hair and brown eyes – she gave a brown impression, more like a woman of forty than a girl of eighteen.' Another Somervillian, Hazel Bishop, described Margaret Roberts in Brenda Maddox's *Maggie* as 'brown haired, plumpish, with a voice that she had worked on and used with great care. She never seemed young.'

A fellow undergraduate, also at Somerville, was Sheila

Browne. She went on to become a distinguished fellow at St Hilda's College in Oxford, where she taught me medieval French and was also my moral tutor. Sheila Browne eventually became the Senior Chief Inspector of Schools and was in that post at the same time as Margaret Thatcher was Education Secretary. It was also the time when I was a schools inspector in Norfolk, and had professional as well as personal contact with Miss Browne. I was intrigued by the fact that she and Margaret Thatcher, who had known each other at Somerville, were now both working in the Department for Education. Miss Browne told me that she and Margaret Thatcher had, when they were undergraduates, shared a bedroom after a dance, but that at that time, Margaret Roberts was not particularly memorable. Miss Browne, as told in John Campbell's book *Margaret Thatcher*, formed the later impression that Margaret Roberts was a 'deeply insecure young woman, concerned above all to do the right thing'. And Janet Vaughan, Principal of Somerville from 1945, explains to John Campbell why she did not invite Margaret Roberts to social occasions at weekends. 'She wasn't interesting, except as a Conservative. If I had interesting or amusing people staying with me, I would never have thought of asking Margaret Roberts – except as a Conservative.' In other words, a not very interesting specimen of an alien and unacceptable breed. Leaving aside this dreadful example of a peculiarly Oxford type of narrow-mindedness, later to flower into the university's decision not to award an honorary doctorate to Britain's first, and so far only, woman Prime Minister, one is forced to conclude that her time at Oxford was not Margaret Thatcher's finest, or happiest, hour.

Even within the embrace of the Oxford University Conservative Association (OUCA), where she was eventually elected president in 1946, a great achievement for a woman, she was not remembered as a brilliant performer, but rather as a very ambitious but conventional political thinker.

What made the difference was her first experience of live politics, as an OUCA representative at the 1946 Conservative Party Conference. She was entranced. For the first time in her adult life, she felt surrounded by people who thought as she did. There was a place for her. She could see her way forward.

By the time she was selected to fight her first seat, Dartford, at the tender age of twenty-three, she was completely transformed. Comments from Dartford voters recalled by the late Bob Dunn included glowing tributes to her looks, her ability, her quickness to answer and her extraordinary capacity for hard work. Others remarked on her capacity for leadership in preparing for her first election campaign, and the sheer energy she devoted to it. Although she, and everyone else, must have known that she could not win such a safe Labour seat, she inspired members of the Association with her own enthusiasm for the fight. During the campaign itself she was absolutely tireless in her preparation for the election, campaigning, canvassing, speaking at meetings, sustained by excitement and her own ambition. She had found her niche. During the election campaign, which in those days featured many public meetings, she drew huge crowds; everyone wanted to see her.

Janet Fookes first encountered the name of Margaret Roberts when she was

> *going out with a young man whose father was one of the leading Conservative agents in the country. Having seen her soundly defeated in a selection procedure, he observed to his son that 'women don't make it in politics'. The next time she hove into my sight it was the early 1960s, and I was at a Conservative lunch in the Queen's Hotel, Hastings. Margaret was the guest speaker, now a thrusting young MP who made a confident speech on the theme of 'Politics is the Art of the Possible'. I reckon this pragmatic approach was to be the distinguishing hallmark of her entire parliamentary career. It was simply that what others thought was impossible, Margaret considered possible.*

There is no doubt that the arrival of Margaret Thatcher, the newly elected MP for Finchley, in the House of Commons in 1959 made an electrifying impact. After all the difficulties she had had to get selected as a woman, once she was elected, she enjoyed an enormous amount of attention from the press and media because she was a woman.

Jill Knight remembers:

Margaret Thatcher's professionalism, attention to detail, immaculate appearance and seemingly indefatigable constitution were all on show during her tour of Norfolk in 1974.

Election day, 1979. Margaret Thatcher's reaction to her historic win is captured in these candid photographs. © Sarah Joiner

TOP Mrs T. in finest attire on a visit to Plymouth. © Baroness Fookes

LEFT An outsider with her insider: Denis and Margaret Thatcher.

BELOW Mrs T. with Gillian Shephard.

A woman in a man's world: Mrs T. is applauded by her Cabinet colleagues, including Nigel Lawson, Geoffrey Howe, Norman Fowler, Tom King, John Major and Douglas Hurd. © Press Association

Paving the way for women in politics: Mrs T. and the female MPs of 1991, featuring Lynda Chalker (left of MT), Janet Fookes (directly behind MT) and Gillian Shephard (far front right). © Peter Beal and John Rifkin

From the very start, she had steadily built up an enviable reputation among colleagues from all parties. Her maiden speech was unique, for she used it to introduce her own Private Member's Bill. She was able to do this because she had gained a top place in the annual ballot for Private Members' Bills, What made her speech doubly memorable was that she went from start to finish without a note.

She was constantly reported in the *Evening Standard*, doing radio and television interviews, being asked about her clothes, her home, her children, her views on anything and everything. One can only imagine how her fellow male colleagues felt about it all. But her charisma was undoubted. The brown girl of the Oxford days had gone, and in her place was a woman whose presence made itself felt as soon she walked onto a platform or into a room. She was full of fervour and passion. Politics had turned her on.

Everyone who has worked with Margaret Thatcher knows how much she relished the challenge and excitement of elections, the long days packed with activity and change, the hourly need for decisions, great or small, and the thrill of campaigning out on the street. There was not a moment to be wasted, she would note with satisfaction, urging everyone, 'Let's get on with it.'

Jean Lucas was a Conservative Party agent, eventually becoming Chairman of the National Society of Agents in 1980. She has kept a record of some of the events in her long and successful professional life, including the by-election in 1975 that saw the Conservative Peter Bottomley elected in West Woolwich. She believes that 'Margaret Thatcher was the first leader to see it as her job to support candidates in by-elections.'

Virginia Bottomley, Peter's wife, also has memories of that by-election and the electrifying part played in it by Mrs Thatcher.

My first encounter with Margaret Thatcher was in 1975 as the dutiful wife of the by-election candidate in West Woolwich. Peter had fought the seat on two previous occasions in 1974. The MP, Bill Hamling, died. Peter had hung on assisting the constituency in the aftermath of the two defeats. Suddenly he found himself fighting the first by-election since Margaret Thatcher's election as party leader. Her arrival in the constituency was full of anxiety and excitement. I walked with her round the streets as a 27-year-old ingénue. She was formidable, intimidating and impressive. The Conservatives, Peter, and Margaret won the by-election.

Sarah Joiner describes Mrs Thatcher's first campaign as leader of the Conservative Party in 1979. She gives a vivid picture of the details of a political campaign and of the powerful leadership given by Mrs Thatcher to every aspect of it.

I was appointed as personal assistant to Roger Boaden, the European Elections Officer at Conservative Central Office (CCO) in February 1979. I was just nineteen. We were co-ordinating the national activities of the candidates for the first direct elections to the European

Parliament. A few weeks after we started working together, Roger came back from a meeting to announce that the general election had been called, and that he was to be the organiser of the leader's election campaign tour. This was because he had previously organised campaign tours for Ted Heath. We gained a deputy for Roger B., another Roger – Roger Pratt, and a second secretary, Jane Pitcher.

It was our job to coordinate every aspect of getting Mrs T. and her entourage around the UK to meet party members and the public, minute by minute during the campaign.

While Mrs T.'s speechwriters and policymakers were in different parts of CCO, we inhabited an eyrie at the top of Smith Square painted in screaming yellow. We also adopted the trio of police officers assigned to Mrs. T.'s personal protection into our already cramped space during the times they were in the building with her. It was unnerving to see their holster guns when they took their jackets off, but you got used to it quite quickly.

Most of my time was spent typing endless sheets of detailed programme notes and checking detail. It was all highly confidential and every copy was numbered and issued only to those on the 'need to know' list. The information literally tracked Mrs T. every minute of the day. I clearly remember typing things like:

'08.01 Door opens at Flood Street'

'08.03 Mrs Thatcher in car, moves off towards...'

We detailed every handover from police force to police force along motorways and at county borders, we scheduled hair appointments, dress fittings, meal breaks, hotel arrangements, the names of key 'meeters and greeters'; everything was listed on the sheets.

On many occasions Mrs T. would come to sit with us in our yellow *offices. She usually came on her own or with only one or two others. She was always cheerful and professional, in that wonderful 'head girl' way, jollying us along when we were about to collapse. Such energy made us determined to keep up. I remember her perching on my desk one evening explaining to me that yellow was just the colour to keep us all awake and motivated. Pale green, she declared, was quite hopeless as it dulled the senses. When I was typing yet more amendments to a speech, she made me a cup of tea.*

I remember Roger B. being cross when we had to change the official cars used to transport Mrs T. The reason was because the car boots were not big enough to lay her dresses out flat inside, to keep them in pristine order. Roger B. went off muttering furiously that this had to be a 'woman thing', as all previous leaders, who of course had been men, just put their suit bag in the boot without a fuss.

During the campaign Mrs T. acquired a coach nicknamed the battle bus, all decked out in party colours. On the day of its delivery to Smith Square, the press were invited to see it in action. As Mrs T. sat on the seat dictating a note to Jane, I bashed away at a typewriter set up on the table between us. The bus slowly circled the square as photographers snapped away.

I was formally introduced much later to Mrs T. at a national rally, and she knew without prompting who I was and what I did. She asked after my parents, Trixie and Kevin Gardner, and if we still had our home in north Cornwall. I was impressed because she always thanked her backroom boys and girls.

Sarah Joiner added in conversation that Mrs Thatcher always packed the sleeves of her dresses and jackets with tissue paper. 'It keeps them in shape, you see. I always do it, and you should, too.'

Harvey Thomas has other memories of the organisation involved in this election campaign.

> All of us who worked on the 'advance party' for Mrs T.'s visits and travel were dedicated to protecting her and projecting her. Sometimes we had to move quickly to stop others taking advantage. On a visit to Alton Towers, we had worked through a very careful route and plan for the whole visit. The Special Branch were of course with us, and everything had been approved for her personal wellbeing, for the political presentation and for security. It was only when I was walking alongside her and the hosts, and realised we were edging in the wrong direction that I quickly spoke to the boss and pointed this out. He said, 'We thought we would take her on the big roller coaster.' I grabbed a Special Branch colleague and together we made it clear that that was not part of the plan, and in the space of twenty to thirty yards we had reverted to the right route. She would have done whatever we arranged, but it would have been very uncomfortable not to say embarrassing for her to be put on a roller coaster, half the time upside down.
>
> I think it was the sense of duty that actually helped her to deal with many situations by just getting on with it. In the 1979 election, during my very early time with her, we were on an election visit to a farm near Ipswich. Before any of us could do anything, the farmer had thrust a baby calf into her arms. Looking back at the video of the occasion, her face takes on a determined look and instinctively she turned to the cameras and said, 'Don't expect me to hold this for twenty minutes while you take pictures.'

Michael Brunson in *A Ringside Seat* sets this occasion in context.

It was clear that this style of campaigning with its heavy emphasis on the photo-opportunity would be used in the election. Our two travelling cameramen never lacked for a picture. The Leader of the Conservative Party tasted chocolates in Birmingham, butter in Aberdeen, and tea without milk or sugar at a tea factory in Newcastle. She had wires stuck all over her as her heart was checked in Milton Keynes and she waved two shopping bags around in Halifax, to show, she said, how much a pound had bought under the Tories six years earlier, and how much less it was now buying under Labour. Most famously of all, she cuddled a calf in a field near Ipswich. It was that last incident which came to symbolise the whole new approach to campaigning. It was all meant to tie in with whatever the theme of the day was supposed to be, presumably something to do with agriculture. But the whole operation seemed so outrageously over the top that it produced plenty of criticism that it was simply a picture for the sake of the picture alone ... Mrs Thatcher not only posed but also began to answer questions with the young animal still clasped to her bosom. In my commentary later, I described the event, with considerable understate-ment and with not a little irony, as probably the first time that a major British politician had ever conducted a news conference in the middle of a field, while holding a farm animal. So agitated did Denis Thatcher become that he was heard to remark, 'If we're not careful, we'll have a dead calf on our hands.' Indeed, for several days afterwards, I and several others of the travelling reporters made regular enquiries about the calf's health, in the hope of an even more spectacular dénouement to the whole business, but it was not to be. The calf, in the true spirit of Thatcherism, survived.

It is interesting to read Michael Brunson's slightly disapproving account of a national figure making such play with photo opportunities in a general election campaign. But Mrs Thatcher and her advisers were in the vanguard of presentational change for political figures. By the time I fought my first parliamentary election in 1987, everyone was doing it. The advice from Conservative Central Office by then was: 'One image is worth a thousand words.'

The 1979 election campaign, which put Mrs Thatcher into No. 10, culminated in another innovation: the first big public election rally at the Wembley Conference Centre. Harvey Thomas describes what happened.

The chairman of the Conservative Party, Lord Thorneycroft, a great man, had, with other party hierarchy figures, decreed that we could not use the song 'Hello Maggie' (to the tune of 'Hello Dolly') at the Wembley rally because it would be infra dig *for the woman who was going to become Prime Minister. We had a fantastic warm-up with many stars well known at the time, and Lulu had been prepared to lead the audience in singing the song 'Hello Maggie'. However, as instructed, I deleted it from the scheduled programme.*

But then Mrs Thatcher was announced and began a walk to the platform and there was another of those split seconds in time when there is total silence and someone yelled out, 'What about the song?'

The time was right. I was standing behind Lulu on the platform, touched her shoulder and said, 'Go.' Another friend, Pete Bye, was sitting at the organ, his eyes professionally glued on me and, as I pointed my finger at him, he struck the first chord of 'Hello Maggie'. What followed, forgive the cliché, is history. The audience sang their hearts out, Mrs T. was almost in tears and people cheered and cheered. It was after that rally, while we were still in the conference centre, that Mrs T. asked me if I would stay on working with her in the whole field of presentation.

Margaret Thatcher loved campaigning, and was at her most energetic dynamic self when she was on the campaign trail. Even so, she was determined to adopt the most professional approach possible to campaigning, and in 1980 sent Harvey and Marlies Thomas to see what the Republicans were doing in the United States.

In 1980, when Ronald Reagan was running for the Republican nomination for President of the United States, Marlies and I were sent over to study the election campaigning techniques in America to see if there was anything that might be adapted for British use. In Victorville, in the Mojave Desert in California, we were introduced to Ronald Reagan, and the three of us sat on a bale of hay backstage, while Roy Rogers and Dale Evans sang to a 10,000 crowd outside on the stage.

Harvey Thomas points out that, on the subject of presentation, Margaret Thatcher expected and accepted professional advice, based, no doubt, on some of the experience he had gleaned in the US. No effort was too great. No detail was too small.

A significant mistake by Neil Kinnock's advisers and the infamous Sheffield Rally in 1992 (at which it was said Kinnock lost that election), was to allow him to make a triumphal entrance walking through the whole length of the arena in Sheffield, so that by the time he reached the platform his mind was on everything but the content of his speech. With Mrs Thatcher, in contrast, we always made sure she had the shortest possible distance from backstage to the lectern, so that her mind could totally concentrate on the content and message she wanted to project.

To help, I would rig a couple of bright 800-watt television lights backstage and for three or four minutes before she went on, she would be looking directly into these lights, so that when she appeared in front of all the television lights on stage, she no longer had to squint. If there was a guest or friend backstage, she would comment to them, 'Harvey likes to blind me before I go on, you know!'

When I introduced the idea to her in the 1983 election, she accepted it immediately and took it for granted that it would help her to be ready for the TV lights on stage.

Introducing the autocue was not quite so straightforward, at least until she saw how effectively Ronald Reagan used it when he spoke to both Houses of Parliament on his visit to the UK. It was quite a major introduction to British speech-making at the time, and, once she agreed to try it, she asked if we could do at least three or four solid rehearsals before she used it for real. And that's what we did. I think there were four separate occasions when we set up the autocue in Downing Street, using some of her old speeches, and she quickly understood its principles and began to use it efficiently.

She also understood the need for careful integration of every aspect of her presentation – not just herself and her speech, and the way she dressed, but positioning the teleprompter screens, lighting and backlighting, positions of cameras, adequate space on the lectern, and microphone at the right height.

In 1985, at the Capitol in Washington, Mrs Thatcher was going to speak to the joint Houses of Congress. Setting things up beforehand, I had an argument with the then Speaker, Tip O'Neill, about whether we could have Mrs Thatcher's favourite mineral water, Ashbourne, on the lectern when she spoke. He claimed it was commercial but common sense won the day, and I had the bottle of Ashbourne on the lectern in good time. After the speech, Tip O'Neill asked the Prime Minister whether she really did like her Ashbourne water as much as I had said. She replied, 'When I see that Ashbourne bottle on the lectern, I know that everything is ready, that the lighting, microphones and teleprompter will all have been properly arranged. That gives me the confidence to focus on the speech.'

I remember when the proceedings of the House of Commons were first televised, in the autumn of 1989.

We ministers were all offered training, perfunctory in the extreme, and which in my case made no difference at all, although most would agree that after a short time, we all forgot the cameras were there. Margaret Thatcher, however, predictably took the innovation very seriously, and was said to have had many rehearsals in the Chamber at the dead of night. The result was that the television news almost always carried sound-bites of Prime Minister's Questions, with her in devastating form.

Despite all this care and attention lavished on the visual media, the written press was still vitally important to politicians at this time. Most Prime Ministers and Cabinet ministers made a point of being in regular contact with key journalists and editors, and were on first-name terms with them. Mrs Thatcher had a less hands-on approach, although her attitude to the media during elections was different, like everything else.

Although Mrs Thatcher seldom saw political journalists at Westminster, Peter Riddell recalls how, during election campaigns, she was very accessible.

That was the era when the leaders of the main parties still saw the need to hold daily news conferences, then in and around Smith Square. She treated these events as seminars, as her daily chance to educate backward political journalists. Each political editor was given his – and it was still largely his rather than her – chance to ask a daily question. Even if the question was addressed to some other minister, she invariably intervened. While the broadcasters sat at the front to catch the cameras, some of us preferred to sit at the back in the crowded room used for press conferences. This was to allow us to hear the comments of Denis Thatcher, who stood at the back with some Conservative Central Office stalwarts. He offered an audible running commentary – 'bloody silly question', 'a leftie' etc. It was the world of Private Eye*'s 'Dear Bill' letters made flesh.*

One day during the 1987 election, I had stayed behind after the Labour Party news conference to raise a point with Neil Kinnock at what is now Local Government House in Smith Square, just across the road from the then Conservative Central Office. When I got over to Central Office, the small news conference room was full, so I watched proceedings on one of the television monitors in the foyer outside, knowing that a couple of my colleagues from the Financial Times *were inside. I was standing there when the press conference finished and Mrs Thatcher came out, accompanied by Norman Tebbit, the party chairman. (No one ever called him the Chair.) She walked up to me and said, in the dismissive tone of the schoolmaster chiding a naughty pupil for not having done his homework, 'You didn't ask your usual question today, Mr Riddell.' I stumbled out with my explanation about following up some point with the Labour leader. She questioned me about this, and then said, 'You'll want to know what happened here, then.' She then gave a summary of what had happened at the Conservative press conference, much to the amusement of Norman Tebbit standing behind her. The truant had to be instructed – a strange but characteristic use of prime ministerial time.*

At the Party Conference, during elections, on the international stage, there was no trace of the 'rather brown unmemorable girl' who had so singularly failed to impress the world of Oxford. Quite simply, politics was her métier, and in it she shone.

The last time I saw her in the House of Commons was the day before William Hague was elected as Leader of the Conservative Party in the summer of 1997. There had been a press conference at the Atrium restaurant at 4 Millbank. Afterwards we all streamed back to the St Stephen's entrance of the House of Commons for a photo call. Margaret Thatcher made a staged exit to join us, sweeping down the steps immaculately dressed and coiffed as usual.

The media were there in force, of course, and in the scrum, the ITN producer, Graham Forrester, squatted on the ground so that his microphone could catch Mrs Thatcher's words of wisdom. Looking down at him at her feet, she said, 'Now, the name's Hague, William Hague, H-A-G-U-E, Hague, are you quite sure you've got that?'

I was then asked to persuade her to come into the Commons Tea Room. 'Yes, dear,' she said, 'but I don't have any money with me.' Charging her for a cup of tea was far from our minds. We swept through the House, with her in the vanguard, and sailed into the Tea Room, to the amazement of the newly elected Labour women MPs clustered there. She went straight up to a male MP, sitting enjoying a quiet cup of tea, and said, 'Now, you must vote for William Hague!' He said, 'I certainly would, but I am a Liberal Democrat.' Nothing daunted, she swept up to another, hidden by a newspaper, snatched away the paper and boomed, 'You do support William, don't you?' The MP in question was Sir Richard Body, who did in fact intend to vote for Hague, but it would have taken a brave man to enter into discussion with her on the subject at that moment.

It was a splendid if slightly farcical episode. But it did remind everyone in the Tea Room that day of just what verve and style she had brought to politics. Margaret Thatcher was on the campaign trail again, and the effect was electrifying.

SEVEN

'ELLE A LES YEUX DE STALIN ET LA VOIX DE MARILYN MONROE.'

§ome commentators have claimed that foreign policy was less congenial to Margaret Thatcher than domestic reform. Whether or not that was the case, she had no choice other than to become deeply involved in foreign policy, as all Prime Ministers have to be. Indeed, public perceptions of her still include the many reports of rows in Europe over the British rebate and national sovereignty, not to mention her relationship with Ronald Reagan, the Falklands conflict and the Iraq War. But it is also the case that her election as leader of the British Conservative Party, of all things, and later as Britain's first woman Prime Minister, created a sensation around the world.

Jean Lucas, a senior Conservative Party agent, visited New Zealand and Australia in 1980, and remembers that 'wherever I went I was questioned about Mrs Thatcher as the first woman Prime Minister'. In an interview with the *New Zealand Herald* of 5 February 1980, she pointed out that just six years earlier, people had said that there would never be a woman Prime Minister in Britain – indeed, Mrs Thatcher said it herself. She added,

> Before Mrs Thatcher, most people believed that women could not reach the higher political positions. But Mrs Thatcher has shown that there is no bar to how far a woman can go. British women are very active politically behind the scenes ... a few years ago the ratio of women to men in the Conservative Party organisation was one to nine. Now it is one to three.

Miss Lucas added that at least ten years were needed to

> get the country back on the rails. I am hopeful this will happen under Mrs Thatcher. She is familiar with the day-to-day problems that people face, and she has a first-class brain.

I also recall that wherever I went, either as a government minister or as an individual, people would ask questions about Mrs Thatcher. In France, graffiti mentioning 'Tatcher' abounded, on bridges, alongside railway lines, and on the sides of derelict buildings, usually in the form of 'A bas Tatcher', or 'Mort a Tatcher', or indeed worse. Conversations always turned to whether I had dealings with her, what she was like, and if she would last. I had a particularly lively exchange with members of a French teachers' union at the time of the Miners' Strike in 1984 and 1985, in which they claimed that this was a struggle to the death – her death. I mildly observed that it might be best to wait and see.

In Egypt and in Uruguay and Paraguay, I was besieged by women at receptions and meetings asking if I knew who were Madame Thatcher's couturiers, hairdressers and visagistes. Disappointingly for them, but fortunately for me, I did not know, but given her notably modest tastes in these areas, a factual answer would have been even more of a disappointment for my questioners. On the street more or less anywhere in the world, children trying out their English would rush up and shout 'Mrs Thatcher, Mrs Thatcher' and later 'Iron Lady', a sobriquet she told Sir Richard Parsons she would like to 'divest' herself of as she considered it 'unhelpful'. In Argentina, where, in late 1993, as Minister of Agriculture, Fisheries and Food, I was the first British minister to visit after our Embassy had reopened following the Falklands conflict, points made on the street about Mrs Thatcher (and indeed many things British) were a little different. Fortunately for me, I was there with a trade delegation, mostly to sell bull semen – which, while it may seem strange to many audiences, was well understood in Argentina, and very obviously nothing to do with territorial interests.

At international gatherings, and especially at EU meetings, her presence hovered over proceedings, and people would say 'But what would your Prime Minister say to that?' or 'How will you tell Mrs Thatcher that?' I could not help but notice that male ministers were particularly persistent with such enquiries.

Peter Riddell writes,

My most vivid memories of her were on overseas trips when she was invariably at her most formidable. In Washington in 1985, shortly after Ronald Reagan's second inauguration, she addressed a joint session of Congress and then hosted a dinner party at the British Embassy with the President as guest of honour to mark the 200th anniversary of diplomatic relations after the Revolutionary War.

Later that evening, while Ronald Reagan was making a typically charming speech, she interrupted and capped one of his anecdotes. Not many people can do that with an American President, but she could, and did. 'There you go, Maggie,' he smiled.

Michael Jopling recalls Margaret Thatcher's first meeting with Mikhail Gorbachev.

I was with her at Chequers when she first met Gorbachev, at that time in charge of Soviet agriculture, but about whom the Foreign Office brief was very thin. It took only hours for her to pronounce, 'This is a man with whom I can do business.' How right she was!

That judgement led to an overseas visit which gave a boost to domestic politics, as Peter Riddell remembers.

In March 1987, in the Soviet Union, she held her talk-in with Mikhail Gorbachev, the prelude to her successful re-election a couple of months later. It was a triumph for her, not least by contrast with the troubled visit to Washington immediately beforehand by Neil Kinnock, which had been undermined by some behind-the-scenes manoeuvring with the Reagan White House by Charles Powell, her foreign affairs Private Secretary. Mrs Thatcher was the conviction leader, the epitome of Western values engaging in vigorous debate with the reforming Soviet leader. Even Stalin might have been impressed. On the final day, in Tbilisi, the capital of Georgia, she looked as unlike a Soviet-era leader as possible, and, with her fur hat, was almost like a Russian empress. As an elderly lady kissed her hand opposite the seminary (now a museum) where Stalin had trained, I remarked to Bernard Ingham beside me within the security cordon that nobody in London would believe the scene. 'It's your bloody job to tell them.' As, indeed, it was. On the crowded and noisy VC10 flying back over the Black Sea and up the Danube, she famously said she would 'go on and on'. Ingham muttered, 'Now I'll never be able to retire.' Hubris is always followed by nemesis, and three-and-a-half years later, he, and she, did.

It was no accident that Margaret Thatcher's visit to Russia made such an impression worldwide. She needed a positive overseas event as a launch platform for the 1987 general election campaign, and her wardrobe had been carefully planned with the help of Margaret King of Aquascutum, who was helping to advise her on clothes at this stage of her premiership.

I clearly remember Margaret Thatcher's appearance during her Moscow visit, which received extensive press coverage in Britain. She wore stunning fur hats, beautifully cut warm Aquascutum coats, and had the bearing of at least a tsarina. She also performed memorably on Soviet television, and aroused enormous interest wherever she went.

On 11 June, she won her third term in government with a majority of 102. I was elected to Parliament in that election.

Margaret Thatcher's premiership had a profound effect in France, where she had constructive relations with both François Mitterand and Jacques Chirac. She wrote of the two French Presidents, 'M. Chirac was blunt, forceful, argumentative, had a sure grasp of detail and a profound interest in economics. M. Mitterand was quieter, more urbane, a self-conscious French intellectual, fascinated by foreign policy, bored by detail, possibly contemptuous of economics. Oddly enough, I liked them both.' She had certainly not liked Mitterand's predecessor, the lofty and snobbish Giscard d'Estaing, who referred to her as 'la fille de l'épicier'. It was one thing for her to vaunt her own background, and quite another to have to put up with condescension from the other side of the Channel. One of her own very senior civil servants told me that she had dreaded her first one-to-one meeting with François Mitterand, which took place over dinner in Downing

Street, but that by the time the French President left, she was glowing.

Geoffrey Howe describes an incident at a difficult EU meeting in Copenhagen in 1987, where it had proved well-nigh impossible to make progress, and where Margaret Thatcher had come to the aid of the French President.

Suddenly, President Mitterand asked for the floor. He spoke gravely. His voice was laden with foreboding. We had come to the end of the road, he said. The brightest hopes had been blighted. The dreams of the founding fathers would turn to dust. Perhaps a community of twelve nations could never be made to work. And so on, for ten minutes or more. This semi-spontaneous epilogue, as may be imagined, cast something of a pall over the proceedings. Then, to my surprise, Margaret Thatcher leaned forward and asked to speak. 'Come on,' she said brightly, 'it isn't as bad as that. We've made a lot of progress. But we haven't finished today. Don't you remember just how gloomy things looked in Brussels in 1984? Yet three months after that, at Fontainebleau, under your brilliant chairmanship, President Mitterand, we did reach a major agreement. And I am quite sure that, under Chancellor Kohl's chairmanship in a few months' time, we can do the same. So' – *very* brightly – 'cheer up, President Mitterand, cheer up!' And President Mitterand, catching the mood of the occasion, replied, 'I begin to wonder whether Madame

Thatcher isn't even more intriguing when she is saying yes than when she is saying no.'

All those present at Copenhagen were indeed heartened by the tone of Margaret's closing remarks. We were still all on the same side, they felt – and I hoped – whatever the difficulties from month to month. This was reflected in the continental press. The French, Italian and Belgian newspapers spoke of Margaret Thatcher's 'good will', portrayed her as 'restrained but firm', and commended the 'clarity and consistency of her views, and particularly the way in which her "soft approach" contributed to showing divisions among others'. It showed very clearly what could be done.

There is no doubt that M. Mitterand was intrigued by *la dame de fer*, whether she was saying yes or no. In August 1992, I had to act as interpreter for him at a private dinner organised to mark the opening of 'the Grove of Albion' in the newly restored garden of the Château de Cormatin, near Cluny. The official opening was performed by the then Archbishop of Canterbury, George Carey, who was staying at Taizé, the well-known Christian evangelical centre in Burgundy. The owners of the château had taken advantage of the presence of the Mitterands on holiday at Mme Mitterand's home in Cluny to invite them to attend in a private capacity. Much to everyone's surprise and pleasure, they accepted, although what followed, perhaps inevitably, was anything but private. The tiny village was invaded by at least eighty of the President's security staff, displacing members of the local *garde champêtre*, who had been in charge of traffic arrangements, and causing the boulangerie to have to reopen as bread supplies ran out. From apparently nowhere there appeared a number of French ministers, including Jack Lang the Culture Minister, and a distinctly carnival atmosphere developed, enhanced no doubt by the copious amounts of marvellous wine which flowed in all directions.

Over dinner, I interpreted for the President and the Archbishop as they engaged in conversation, but in the interstices, M. Mitterand was questioning me closely about Mrs Thatcher. How had her downfall come about? Were British politicians mad to get rid of such an outstanding Prime Minister? What role had the Queen played in all this – surely she could have prevented such a disaster? (A question I thought particularly rich from a Republican.) Who was her couturier? Did I understand that such a thing could never happen in France, the constitution specifically prevented such a thing, and why did the British not have such constitutional arrangements? What did I think of her husband, and what kind of man could be married to such a woman? It went on and on, interrupted from time to time by the Archbishop asking what the President was talking about, and Jack Lang capering about taking photographs of the occasion. I was not prepared to gossip with the President about Mrs Thatcher, at least partly because I did not know the answers to most of his extremely indiscreet questions, and eventually, but with no less enthusiasm, he turned to discussion of the Duchess of York. Photographs of her on holiday in the south of France had appeared in *Paris Match* that summer, apparently having her toes sucked by a lover. Fortunately, when we reached this stage, it was time for us to leave the table for the opening of the Grove of Albion, to which we all proceeded, more or less steadily, according to the amount of wine we had enjoyed.

Dr Sophie Loussouarn, a distinguished French academic and commentator on British politics and the British economy, interviewed, for this book, Hubert Védrine who was Mitterand's diplomatic adviser from 1981 to 1988. He was appointed Conseiller d'État and Head of Staff at the Élysée Palace from 1991 to 1995, and was Foreign Secretary in the Jospin government from 1997 to 2002.

Dr Loussouarn gives Védrine's reflections on Mrs Thatcher, and describes the relationship between her and Mitterand and Chirac, while also drawing on the memoirs of Jacques Attali, adviser to M. Mitterand, who became the first President of the European Bank of Reconstruction and Development in London.

When Margaret Thatcher became Prime Minister in 1979, Jean-Marie le Pen was the only French politician who paid tribute to her and welcomed 'the first victory over impoverishing socialism'. Later, her championing of capitalism and her monetarist revolution caused her to be a role model for other French politicians, including Léotard, Madelin and Balladur. But when Mitterand became President of

France on 10 May 1981, thanks to Communist votes, he was deter-
mined to improve relations with European countries, and he was
the first head of state to call Mrs Thatcher to express support in
the Falklands War. There was good mutual understanding between
President Mitterand and the Iron Lady on the Falklands, their attitude
to Gorbachev, and on the Channel Tunnel. But there were antagonisms
between the two over the European budget, the Common Agricultural
Policy and German reunification.

The first meeting between Margaret Thatcher and President
Mitterand took place ahead of the wedding of Prince Charles and
Lady Diana Spencer. The French President wanted to have a good
relationship with Britain, to avoid a right-wing coalition between
the UK and the US. The Iron Lady enjoyed François Mitterand's
culture and finesse, and got on well with him. The disagreements
between Thatcher and Mitterand over Europe mattered less than
their mutual understanding. Besides, in 1981, Europe was not
Mitterand's priority.

The first Franco-British summit took place in London on 10 September
1981, a few months after Mitterand's election as President. Mitterand
and Thatcher discussed Europe and the Common Agricultural Policy
(CAP). Margaret Thatcher reasserted the importance of the EU for
Britain, but underlined the problems of the CAP. She wanted her money
back, as she constantly repeated. Mitterand felt that she did not share the
values of the European community, but praised the commercial genius of
Britain, and called for cooperation between the two countries in computer
engineering. This summit saw the start of the Channel Tunnel project,
which ended Britain's isolation as an island and linked it to continental
Europe. On the plane back to Paris, President Mitterand spoke to his

adviser, Jacques Attali, about Margaret Thatcher, saying, 'She has Stalin's eyes and Marilyn Monroe's voice.'

[President Mitterand is more frequently quoted as describing Margaret Thatcher as having 'the eyes of Caligula and the mouth of Marilyn Monroe', which apparently he also said.]

When the Falklands War broke out, Mitterand at once understood that the honour of the British nation was at stake and that international law should prevail over the use of force. On 3 April 1982, he was the first Western leader to telephone Margaret Thatcher to express his support for the United Kingdom after Argentina's invasion of the Falklands on 2 April. Mitterand was born during the First World War in 1916 and he strongly disapproved of Argentina's attack, believing that frontiers should be safeguarded. In this he differed from his Foreign Secretary, Claude Cheysson, who wanted to back Third World countries against developed nations. According to Védrine, Mitterand's position was 'one of principle: he was neither an atlanticist nor pro-Thatcher, but he disapproved of the military policy of the Argentinians.

'Mitterand did not break off diplomatic relations with Argentina, but he did his very best to help Britain, and supported Britain at the United Nations.' Margaret Thatcher wrote in her memoirs, 'I was to have many disputes with President Mitterand in later years, but I never forgot the debt we owed him for his personal support on this occasion and throughout the Falklands crisis. France used her influence in the UN to swing others in our favour.'

The British attack started on 24 and 25 April and military operations lasted until June. Had Mitterand been in Margaret Thatcher's place, he told Jacques Attali that he would have sent in the whole French

Navy. On 5 April, he confessed to Attali, 'Do I admire Mme Thatcher, or do I envy her?' The answer came when she forced him to give the codes of the French-made missiles, especially the Exocets, to disable Argentina during the conflict. The Falklands War marked a high point in Franco-British relations. During a state visit to the Ivory Coast on 23 May 1982, Mitterand reasserted France's support for Britain. 'Our solidarity to Great Britain must never be questioned. It is our first duty. Yet France must try as much as it can to maintain its friendships, its interests and this historic community which binds her to Latin America. France will always be in favour of peace and against the infringement of the law. France will do its utmost to stop the fighting as soon as possible. But we will not surrender to either Britain or Argentina. We will fight for the restoration of peace which is a pillar of French foreign policy.'

On 1 June 1982, the French President welcomed Margaret Thatcher to the Élysée. They discussed the Falklands, subsidies to Eastern countries, relations with the USSR and Beijing. Mitterand reasserted the importance of Franco-British relations: 'Solidarity with Great Britain is one of the major elements of stability for France in the tumultuous world we live in.' When Britain defeated Argentina in the Falklands War, Mrs Thatcher asked European nations to maintain their economic sanctions as long as Argentina refused to accept defeat. Once again, Mitterand supported her.

Accord on many defence matters was a feature of later Franco-British summits between Mitterand and Thatcher. They discussed nuclear weapons and future relations with the USSR. At their last full summit, at Waddesdon Manor in May 1990, they finally agreed on strengthening Franco-British cooperation on defence. This paved the way for the eventual Franco-British defence agreement in 2011.

The agreement to construct the Channel Tunnel was another significant accord between President Mitterand and Mrs Thatcher. The signing ceremony by the two leaders took place, picturesquely, in the chapter house of Canterbury cathedral in 1986, but the final ratification by Britain and France had to wait until after the 1987 British general election. It was a great political achievement for Margaret Thatcher and François Mitterand.

It was not such a harmonious picture on the EU front, however.

The British contribution to the EU was the major stumbling block between Margaret Thatcher and François Mitterand. The Iron Lady wanted her money back, and in 1983 would not accept the Athens agreement, which increased the European budget by 10 per cent, insisting on a renegotiation of the treaty. She demanded £1.25 billion a year, whereas Mitterand could only accept £1 billion. It was difficult to find a compromise, although Mitterand increased his offer of support to £1.1 billion. In the end, and under the French presidency of the EU, Mrs Thatcher got a 65 per cent rebate. She wrote, 'The rebate I had won had limited our net contribution from rising to a totally unacceptable level, but several of our community partners now wanted to cut or eliminate it.'

After 1984, Margaret Thatcher was prepared to accept enlargement of the EU to include Spain and Portugal. But she rejected the idea of a European monetary and fiscal policy, and that of a European Central Bank. She was totally against the idea of a European super-state exercising power from Brussels, and wanted nation states to retain their sovereignty. She opted out of the Social Chapter at the European council meeting in Strasbourg in December 1989. Mitterand described her personality as 'a mixture of spiritual strength and strategic subtlety'.

Was it because M. Mitterand was French that he was able to discern subtlety in Margaret Thatcher's approach to Europe? In any event, Conservative newspapers like *The Sun* and the *Telegraph* were not inclined to describe it that way: headlines like 'Maggie says no', and even the infamous 'Up Yours Delors' abounded, leaving the British reader in no doubt about the Prime Minister's stance on Europe.

Another area of disagreement between the two leaders was German reunification. Margaret Thatcher feared German reunification, whereas Mitterand set his conditions for a peaceful, democratic process, and it was a deal between him and the German Chancellor, Helmut Kohl. Mrs Thatcher wrote in her diary, 'The immediate effect, through the prospect and then the reality of German reunification, was to strengthen the hand of Chancellor Kohl and fuel the desire of President Mitterand and M. Delors for a federal Europe which would bind in the new Germany to a structure within which its preponderance would be checked.'

During the European Council meeting in Strasbourg in December 1989, the members of the European Community discussed the issue of German reunification. President Mitterand pressed for the creation of a European Bank of Reconstruction and Development (EBRD) in order to channel new investments and assistance to the emerging democracies. Margaret Thatcher was sceptical about this, but she made a deal with Mitterand that the bank would be situated in London, and that his adviser, Jacques Attali, would be its first President. She was keen to slow down German reunification and thought that only an Anglo-French initiative could stop it. She wrote, 'The last and best hope seemed to be the creation of a solid Anglo-French political axis which would ensure that at each stage of reunification – and in future economic and political developments – the Germans did not have things all their own way.'

Douglas Hurd, who became Foreign Secretary in 1989, describes Mrs Thatcher's approach to German reunification:

Only on one subject did I find her resolute and wrong, and that was in her opposition to German unification. On this, the Americans were against her, and so were the French, although President Mitterand did his best to equivocate. On this subject we were lucky to avoid a damaging breakdown. Our arguments brought out another trait in the Prime Minister's character: she dearly liked to have academic backing for what she had in mind. But the cohorts she gathered at Chequers to give her support in a famous seminar proved unwilling to back her in her scathing analysis of the German character.

(This seminar was held at Chequers in March 1990, soon after the Berlin Wall came down. Its discussions were widely leaked to the press. According to Hugo Young, as a result of the seminar, Mrs Thatcher 'withheld her approval of reunification until well past the date when a concession to realism would have been better advised'.)

On her last visit to Paris, on 20 November 1990, and already knowing that she had failed to win outright a leadership vote within the Conservative Party, Margaret Thatcher discussed Iraq and Kuwait with President Mitterand. They failed to agree, but she continued to pursue an Anglo-French entente as a counterbalance to German influence.

When she stepped down, President Mitterand paid generous tribute to her, saying that 'she had played a historic role in Great Britain and in Europe', and that he greatly admired her courage and determination. 'She was an opponent but she had a vision. In the end, I got on very well with her.'

To the Briton in the street, Margaret Thatcher's approach to foreign affairs was defined by her attitude to Europe. Her successor, John Major, who had also served as her Foreign Secretary, gives a sensitive analysis of her line on Europe in his autobiography:

> For most of her time in government, her actions showed the Prime Minister to be as much a pragmatist over Europe as she was a sceptic: she tested new ideas to destruction before she accepted them, but accept them she very often did. Though many thought her line on Europe too abrasive, few disagreed with the decisions she ultimately took. She was unpersuaded on the need for a single currency,

but was prepared to accept, even welcome, integration on issues such as the single market. Overall, the Prime Minister was undeniably 'on board' the European train, even though she was uneasy about where it was heading and complained loudly at every stop.

The trouble was that there was another Margaret Thatcher, usually confined to private quarters, whose gut reaction was much more hostile to Europe. She bridled at the very mention of Brussels, and was thought by many to share the views on Germany which Nick Ridley was quoted expressing in a *Spectator* interview in July 1990, and which were so intemperate he was forced to leave the Cabinet; he resigned, it was said, but in fact he did so at Margaret's request conveyed through Charles Powell. He was effectively sacked. Nick was unlucky. He told me he had made his remarks privately after the end of the interview – but they were printed anyway, and they destroyed him. Margaret's view was equally direct: 'Never trust the Germans.' Two world wars, she thought, proved that the country was expansionist by instinct. Britain's role was to stop it.

The two Margarets could co-exist. They did for most of her premiership to great effect. But, after ten years in power, she began to lose her knack of keeping the two sides of her personality bolted together. It can be a terrible error to argue straight from your emotional bedrock, but the Prime Minister was beginning to do so; like a shorting circuit she flickered and crackled. Intermittently the lamp of European statesmanship still glowed; then – fssst – and a shower of vivid commentary would light up the Margaret who attracted the last-ditch Englander.

EIGHT

'SHE WAS FORCED TO BEHAVE LIKE AN OUTSIDER FOR THE SIMPLE REASON THAT SHE WAS ONE.'

One of the most intriguing features of Margaret Thatcher as Prime Minister was the fact that she was, so patently, not 'one of us'. She obviously relished the image of herself swimming against the tide of the Establishment, as 'the rebel head of an Establishment government', as she put it at a Downing Street reception. Many Prime Ministers see themselves like this: John Major, certainly, and probably also Tony Blair. Indeed, it must often seem that way when you are confronted with Cabinet colleagues, each with his or her own agenda, and a party that opposes change. But with Margaret Thatcher it went deeper than that. She wrote in *The Path to Power*, 'I was often portrayed as an outsider who by some odd mixture of circumstances had stepped inside and stayed there for eleven-and-a-half years; in my case the portrayal was not inaccurate.'

She was most definitely not 'born to rule'. Her origins as the daughter of a Methodist shopkeeper in an East Midlands provincial town, her state education at primary and secondary level, the fact that she read a science subject at Oxford and (worse still, coming from her background) was, unexpectedly, a Conservative – all of this meant that she could not easily be categorised or 'placed' by those in the various worlds into which she climbed, except perhaps by giving her the catch-all status of 'outsider'. Even Ted Heath, like her a product of a grammar school education, and from a humbler background than hers, had 'had a good war', and thus was easier to pigeon-hole.

In fact in Grantham, at the time when Margaret Thatcher was growing up, the Roberts family were anything but outsiders. They must have been regarded by others as both well-to-do and powerful. Her father was self-made. He left school at thirteen and, through careful management, hard work and a thrifty approach, saved enough to buy first one grocery shop and then another. The family had help in the house and even a maid, before the war. Mrs Roberts was a gifted seamstress and tailoress, so the two girls, Margaret and Muriel, her older sister, were always beautifully and smartly turned out. Margaret had piano lessons and was sent, not to the primary school closest to the Roberts home, but to a better one some little distance away. At ten years old she won a scholarship to the

fee-paying girls' grammar school, Kesteven and Grantham
Girls' School. The scholarship was means tested, so Alfred
Roberts had to pay the rest of the fees; her sister Muriel
had also attended the school and presumably fees were
paid in her case, too. The school had a uniform, some
items of which would have had to be bought, not made.
The family took regular holidays, although separately as
the shops could not be left, even though a total of four
workers were employed.

Margaret Thatcher never sought to present her early life
and background as a rags-to-riches story, for the simple
reason that it was not one. She did, however, consistently
express gratitude for what her upbringing had taught her.
In fact, her family's position in Grantham could certainly
have been described as middle class, if she or they had
wished to make such a claim. What is interesting about it is
the sheer ignorance of small-town dynamics displayed by
those of her former colleagues and the many commentators who seek to sneer at her origins, because, as she wrote
in *The Path to Power*:

'Life over the shop' is much more than a phrase. It is
something which those who have lived it know to be quite
distinctive. For one thing, you are always on duty. People
would knock on the door at almost any hour of the night
or weekend if they ran out of bacon, sugar, butter or eggs.
Everyone knew that we lived by serving the customer; it
was pointless to complain, and so nobody did.

In addition, one of the shops was a post office, and its franchise was an important part of Alfred Roberts's business. There would have been in the shop a branch of the Post Office Savings Bank, and elderly people would have visited weekly to get their pension. 'As grocers,' she wrote, 'we knew something about the circumstances of our customers.'

The sum total of all of this is that Margaret Thatcher had, from an early age, first-hand experience of a wide social range of people, and a knowledge of their circumstances that those 'born to rule' could never acquire, imprisoned as they are, from cradle to grave, in their own social class. It was certainly a better preparation for a future politician. This could have been one reason why she found the effortless superiority of the 'born to rule' politician so unutterably exasperating. And why she said, in an interview in the *Sunday Times*, 3 August 1980, 'Deep in their instincts, people find what I am saying and doing is right. And I know it is, because that is the way I was brought up. I'm eternally grateful for the way I was brought up in a small town. We knew everyone, we knew what people thought.'

Her remarkable father's outstanding career in public life must also have given her a broad view, not only of local government, but also of the structure, workings and organisations of a small-town community, impossible to acquire for those coming from a supposedly more sophisticated metropolitan background. It must certainly have given her a vicarious taste of power, since, at the zenith of his public career, Alderman Roberts had an influential finger in many Grantham pies. He was a powerful man.

He was elected an independent councillor to the Grantham Borough Council in 1925. Later, in 1936, he became chairman of the Finance and Rating Committee, a very powerful position in local government. He served a term as Mayor of Grantham in 1946 and was made an Alderman. As a local sub-postmaster, he played a key role during the war, in charge of pensions and military payments and dealing with other emergency arrangements. In addition to this, he was chairman of the local branches of the Chamber of Trade, the Rotary Club and the Workers' Education Association. He was a director of the Trustee Savings Bank and a governor both of the Kesteven and Grantham Girls' Grammar School and of the King's School, Grantham, a long-established boys' grammar school. He was a senior figure in the Finkin Street Wesleyan Methodist Chapel, where the family attended services twice every Sunday, a lay preacher and a trustee of at least ten other local Methodist churches. There is no indication that Alderman Roberts did anything other than fulfil his public duties with dedication and honour in every respect. Indeed, in the goldfish bowl of public life in a small provincial town, he would not have lasted long had his conduct not been above reproach. But the talk in the Roberts household must have been interesting and highly varied, given the number of organisations in which Alderman Roberts had an interest, the wide range of people who came in and out of the shops every day, and the challenge of making a living in trade with all its changing circumstances. Margaret Thatcher had, therefore, from her earliest years, an insight into many aspects of life denied to children above or below her on the social scale. As she said, 'Living over the shop, children see far more of their parents than in most other walks of life. I saw my father at breakfast, lunch, high tea and supper. We had much more time to talk than some other families, for which I have always been grateful.'

For a future politician, such an upbringing and childhood would be a great advantage. However, it was not seen as such by those who liked to patronise the grocer's daughter, many of them in the Conservative Party. It was commonly recounted in the House of Commons that some Tory grandee had described the party to his friends in the City as being like a cavalry regiment led by a WRAC corporal. Unsurprisingly, Margaret Thatcher never took to the grandee element in the party.

Willie Whitelaw, himself the grandest of grandees, served Margaret Thatcher with the utmost loyalty. But even he, after he had left office, admitted that he would never have dreamt of socialising with the Thatchers.

Small wonder then, that after a hostile press conference much later in her career, she remarked to Bernard Ingham: 'The thing about you and me, Bernard, is that neither of us are smooth people.' She might have added, 'And nor are we One of Them.'

When she went up to Oxford, she would have been justified in a certain pride in her achievement. No one in her immediate family had been to either Oxford or Cambridge. To win a place at seventeen years old, as she did, was a great achievement. Nor should she have found her background any kind of handicap: there would have been plenty of clever grammar school girls like her at Somerville. She was nice-looking, hard-working and diligent, and yet at the start she found Oxford 'cold and strangely forbidding'.

She was not given to self-pity, then or at any time later in her career, and threw herself into her work as a scientist, into church activities, music and, of course, politics. But at Oxford, it was her choice of party that made her an outsider. Much of the comment from her contemporaries of the time focuses on the fact that she did not seem to talk about much else apart from the Conservative Party. She was certainly not frivolous or given to undergraduate larks. The fact is that scientists at Oxford, certainly in the late 1950s when I was there, and probably to this day, spent much of their time out of college at the labs. They therefore tended to eat and socialise together, rather than mix with those reading humanities subjects. They also had to do a fourth year of study before taking their final exams, so their rhythm of work was different. But the views of those at Oxford with her, tutors or undergraduates, were given after she had become Prime Minister, and political antipathy may have affected their later pronouncements. At the

very least, their judgements seem remarkably untouched by
any kind of academic detachment. Take the comments of
Dame Janet Vaughan, Principal of Somerville for part of
the time Margaret Roberts was there. 'She was a perfectly
adequate chemist. I mean nobody thought anything of
her. She was a perfectly good second-class chemist, a
beta chemist.' The Nobel Prize winner Professor Dorothy
Hodgkin thought well enough of her to invite her to be a
research assistant in her fourth year, and said, 'I came to
rate her as good. One could always rely on her producing a sensible, well-read essay.' But of course, Margaret
Roberts's real sin was to be a Conservative. That was the
reason that she was not invited to Dame Janet's social
occasions at weekends and why some of her fellow undergraduates recall her as 'unmemorable' or as 'someone who
was never young'. For them, that she dared to be different
from them was the unforgivable sin.

And so history repeated itself, in the famous episode in
1984, when her old university refused to give her – the first
and, so far, the only woman to become Prime Minister of
Britain – the honorary degree they had awarded to Attlee,
Macmillan, Heath, Wilson, Douglas-Home and Eden.
The opposition was led by a committee of 275 objectors
to the award, on the grounds that Margaret Thatcher had
done irremediable damage to the cause of education and,
in particular, higher education. This was undoubtedly the
view of some; my own view of their collective motivation,
however, has been for ever influenced by a very senior don

gleefully telling me, at a college high table a few years later, that, 'Oxford hadn't had so much fun for years.' Oxford's reputation was not enhanced by its stance; I believe that the general public thought it petty, small-minded and politically motivated, and I regretted that my old university should apparently not care about the impression given by its stance. Margaret Thatcher's public response was dignified. She said, 'If they do not wish to confer the honour, I am the last person who would wish to receive it.' Privately, the episode did not reinforce her enthusiasm for the Establishment.

It was wonderfully summed up, in a typically double-edged way, by a remark of Harold Macmillan to Roy Jenkins in 1985, here reported in Anthony Kenny's *A Life in Oxford*.

> Terrible business, Roy, this insult to the Prime Minister by our old University, terrible. You know, it's really a question of class. The dons are mainly upper middle class, and they can never forgive Mrs Thatcher for being so lower middle class. But you and I, Roy, with our working-class ancestry, are above that kind of thing.

She once startled Sir Anthony Parsons, her foreign affairs adviser, by saying to him, 'Do you know, Tony, I am so glad I don't belong to your class.' 'What class would that be, Prime Minister?' Parsons replied. 'The upper middle class who see everybody's point of view but have no view of their own.' This exchange, recorded by Peter Hennessy in *The Prime Minister*, is extremely revealing of her whole attitude to the class hierarchy in Britain.

She appeared to have no time at all for the whole Establishment, the traditional ruling elite. She gave the impression of wanting to take them all on: the BBC, Oxford and Cambridge, the civil service, especially the Foreign Office, and the state-funded professional classes. She had a strong distaste for local government, which might seem surprising given her own father's eminent town hall career; on the other hand, she may have been shocked, as were most people with any kind of regard for the democratic process, by the fact that immediately after the 1979 general election, which she won handsomely, some militant-controlled councils announced that they would challenge the result. We used to sit in the House of Commons Tea Room, gloomily reckoning up all the interest groups her government, and ours for that matter, had offended and wondering quite how this might play out at the polls. Not that it seemed to matter to her. No one could have been less concerned with political popularity.

This iconoclastic disregard for the conventions certainly extended to the management of her Cabinet and her attitude to the civil service, even to other ministers' special advisers (although not to her own). On occasion, she actually seemed to take the view that she was nothing to do with her own government – or 'the government' as she sometimes used to refer to it – and that one of her roles was to protect the public from it. Compared with all her successors, she enjoyed very favourable press coverage, but, far from being grateful, she treated even the most well-respected journalists with disdain.

Her attitude to Parliament was somewhat different. Michael Brunson writes in *A Ringside Seat* that she told him 'Parliament could hold up her plans for a year, but no more', which implies that she had a healthy respect for the conventions and role of Parliament, and nothing more than that. She was certainly not clubbable, and regarded the Commons as a place of work, a place in which to perform, but not one in which to spend all one's waking hours. When she first became an MP, she had young children and a busy home and constituency life, and would certainly have left the House promptly after votes.

For that reason, some have claimed that she was a bit of an outsider in Parliament too. But when I was a back-bencher and junior minister during her time as Prime Minister, my impression was that she took great care over her relations with the House of Commons. She was very frequently in the Commons, as statistics confirm. For one thing, she voted in more than 30 per cent of divisions when she was Prime Minister. Tony Blair voted in about 5 per cent. Milburn Talbot, Head Doorkeeper in the Commons, recalls her coming in most evenings, after some outside engagement, to vote, to have meetings in her room behind the Speaker's Chair, or to be around, 'always marvellously dressed in a long gown, and wafting clouds of perfume.

She always had a word for the doorkeepers and the police-men.' I think she enjoyed the atmosphere of repartee and gossip. Allan Rogers, the former Labour MP for the Rhondda, not exactly a fellow traveller, enjoyed paying her extravagant compliments on her appearance, to which she used to reply, 'You Welsh, you're such flatterers!'

She would regularly go into the less salubrious cafeterias and into the Members' Dining Room to eat and chat to people. Sometimes she would appear in the Strangers' Dining Room, and I can remember my stepson being struck dumb by her sudden appearance at our table. On one occasion, I remember her coming into the Tea Room during an all-night sitting at around 5 a.m., where we were slouching, unwashed and bleary-eyed, around a table on which were the remains of the night's teas, coffees and sandwiches. 'You've been eating buns,' she cried accus-ingly. No one had the courage or energy to argue, although there were points that might have been made.

Janet Fookes has a very positive memory of Mrs Thatcher's attendances in the Commons.

> When she was Prime Minister, I noticed the frequency with which she would be voting in the division lobbies late into the evening, even if her crowded itinerary meant that she was getting up early the next day, often on a gruelling overseas visit. It was clear that she had a strong sense of duty towards the House of Commons as an institution, and a concern that she did not expect members of her party to be voting when she had chickened out.

Ian Beesley recounts her cautious attitude towards the role of Parliament.

> *She was sensitive to the mood and will of the House of Commons. The Rayner/Efficiency Unit wanted to conduct a study of the costs imposed on government by Parliament through parliamentary questions, briefing for debates, appearances at Select Committees etc. She would not entertain the idea; it was not the job of the government to scrutinise Parliament.*

Both Michael Jopling in his role as Chief Whip and Patrick Cormack as an influential backbencher recall that she was sufficient of an insider to encourage the playing of parliamentary games within the House of Commons.

Michael Jopling writes,

> *After the 1979 election, she announced her whole ministerial team on the Sunday evening, following polling day on the Thursday. Over a drink that evening, I said that she had not yet invited anyone to be her Parliamentary Private Secretary. She asked me if I had any ideas. 'Would you buy Ian Gow?' I offered. She readily agreed, and when I phoned him he asked if eight o'clock would be a suitable time for him to report at No. 10 the following morning. 'I think nine o'clock would be more appropriate,' I suggested.*
>
> *I think that history has not reflected the influence that Ian Gow had on Margaret Thatcher over the next four years. For instance, I have always felt that his strong eurosceptic views drew her more and more into that position over the early years of government.*

She turned a blind eye to some of Ian's activities in causing mischief by encouraging dissent to causes which were close to his and her heart, although contrary to the government's policy. An example was the difficulty we had in passing Jim Prior's Northern Ireland Bill, which was unpopular with some of our own members and Enoch Powell, who was then an Ulster Unionist MP. In the end, I had to tell her that it was taking so long that we must move a timetable motion. [Michael Jopling means by this that Conservative MPs had been holding up the progress of their own government's Bill by filibustering, or making over-long speeches, raising unnecessary points of order and so on, and encouraged to do so by the Prime Minister's own PPS.] She said, 'I hope you realise, Michael, that you are the first Chief Whip to move a guillotine motion against our own side?' But she agreed.

Deep waters indeed.

Patrick Cormack recalls another covert operation when Margaret Thatcher was Leader of the Opposition.

Most of my memories of this time are associated with a small and rather unusual dining group I convened. For many months I used to meet Reg Prentice, at that time Minister for Overseas Development in the Callaghan government, almost on a weekly basis, after Cabinet meetings and we would have lunch together at the Reform Club (in Pall Mall). It became increasingly clear that he was not only disenchanted by his supremely unattractive constituency party in Newham, but he was also less and less in sympathy with the Labour government of which he was a member and with the Prime Minister who had appointed him. It was out of these meetings that we formed a little coterie. It consisted of three Labour and three Tory MPs. The other Labour members were John Mackintosh and Brian Walden, and the Tories were Julian Amery, his brother-in-law Maurice Macmillan and me. Being the most junior, I acted as organiser / secretary.

Even now, I will not give the full inside story of that remarkable episode in late 1970s political life. Sufficient to say that we formed a line of communication to the Leader of the Opposition. Brian Walden met her from time to time, and even helped to draft some of her speeches. And I took Reg to see her at her home in Flood Street, both before and after he left the government. It did not take long after he had returned to the backbenches for him to join the Conservative Party. He was adopted to fight the safe seat of Daventry at the next election. In our meetings, Margaret showed herself very alive to the dramatic possibili- ties produced by the conversion of a Labour Cabinet minister to the Tory cause. She also saw the attraction of working closely with those in other parties and made some of her own approaches, sometimes assisted by us. One in particular was to Roy Jenkins. Reg himself was given an assurance that he would be in any future Conservative government, and both he and we thought that would mean a Cabinet position. Another by-product was a book of essays by new converts from the left, which I edited. Entitled Right Turn, *its leading piece was by Reg.*

After the 1979 general election, he was made Minister for the Disabled, outside the Cabinet. Having played a fairly significant part in orchestrating his defection, I was somewhat disappointed that there was no place for me in the first Thatcher government.

[In fact, Patrick Cormack was approached by the late Jack Weatherill to see if he would like to become a Whip, but Patrick

turned down the offer, in what he describes as 'possibly the most
mistaken decision of my political life'.]

Margaret Thatcher herself would have made no claims to
be the kind of orator whose speeches filled the Chamber
of the House of Commons. Indeed, I heard her say on
many occasions, 'If you want a speech made, ask a man. If
you want something done, ask a woman.'

Peter Riddell confirms that:

She was never a natural orator. She was always rather awkward and
obviously uneasy with the artifices of speech writers. Her success came
from the power of her personality, the force of the conviction politician,
the sabre rather than the rapier. Hence her most memorable speeches
were all about the circumstances – the Iron Lady being tested during the
Falklands conflict or in the aftermath of the Brighton bomb in October
1984. On both these occasions, it was less the soon-to-be forgotten words
that impressed than the expression of the personal will of the leader.

I believe that she had strong respect for the conventions of
Parliament. She may not have been a devotee of the gossipy
Tea Room and bars, but she knew how much backbenchers mattered. Tellingly, she writes in *The Downing Street Years*
about the afternoon of her first Cabinet meeting:

In all this activity of government making and policy
setting, however, I knew I could not neglect the backbenchers. After twenty years in the House of Commons, through

six parliaments, I had seen how suddenly trouble could
arise and the business of the House be put in jeopardy. So
on the Tuesday evening, before Parliament assembled the
following day, I had invited the chairman and officers of
the 1922 Committee for a talk to celebrate our victory and
discuss the work of the coming parliamentary session ...
Even in less stormy times, a heavy legislative programme is
only possible when there is a good working understanding
between No. 10, the 1922 Committee, the Whips' Office
and the Leader of the House.

And she knew very well that it was the Commons that had
the power to make a party leader – and to destroy a party
leader. Patrick Cormack recalls the events which led up to
her election as Leader of the Conservative Party.

*I had no personal dealing with her during those rather fraught years
of the Heath administration, which was brought to a shuddering halt
when he made the fatal mistake of asking the country who ran it, in
the second Miners' Strike. I was one of those who spoke out against
a premature election. Although Heath won more votes than Harold
Wilson's Labour Party, he was out, and an unhappy leader of an
increasingly fractious party during the months leading up to the second
1974 election in October.*

*When Ted Heath failed again, it was quite clear that his days
were numbered. All over the Palace of Westminster, one would find
Conservatives talking of, and often plotting for, a change at the top.
I was one of a small group, convened by Nigel Fisher and Airey*

Neave, who talked of various potential successors. Keith Joseph had ruled himself out by a rather injudiciously worded speech. Incredibly, Edward du Cann was briefly considered, and then one night Airey Neave came along, looking particularly conspiratorial, and said, 'What about Maggie?' It was the first time I had heard her called that. Initially his suggestion was met with almost total scepticism but, as it became increasingly clear that she was the only politician of any real stature who might have the courage to allow her name to go forward, we coalesced around her and the bandwagon began to roll.

The rest, as they say, is history, but I had my own ringside seat. I was leading a small deputation from the National Association of Widows, including Eve Macleod, its president (the widow of Iain Macleod), and June Henner, the founder and chairman, who happened to come from Staffordshire, to see the Leader of the Conservative Party. The date fixed was after the first ballot and before the second, and so it was the Acting Leader, Robert Carr, we saw. And we saw him on the very afternoon that the second ballot was declared. Indeed, our meeting was interrupted by a phone call giving the result and, when he came back from taking it, he handed a piece of paper to Eve Macleod and me, announcing Margaret Thatcher's triumph. 'Well, she ought to be sympathetic to widows,' was Eve's immediate response.

Later that evening, Airey Neave hosted a celebration party for those of us who had taken part in the campaign and, at a suitable moment, Margaret herself arrived, with a broad but determined smile and an immediate pep talk.

That was a dramatic enough Westminster event, but it was nothing compared with the night of 28 March 1979, when Jim Callaghan lost the vote of confidence in the Commons, clearing the way for a general election and allowing Margaret Thatcher to get her hands on the reins of power.

Jill Knight was there.

None of us who were MPs at the time will ever forget 28 March 1979. Britain had just been through the Winter of Discontent. Militants in the trade unions were holding the country to ransom and just about everybody was on strike. Birmingham's car industry was being strangled by a rabid union leader known as Red Robbo. Constituents of mine who worked in the factories he controlled told me of the beating-up of any man who voted against strike action. The atmosphere of fear was tangible. Factories which made other goods were also strike-bound, but the local authority still demanded taxes from them, as long as the building was useable. So the owners took the roofs off them and I shall never forget how bleak those gaunt, headless buildings looked when I drove past. Miners, schools, street cleaners, dustmen, even grave diggers, were on strike.

For Margaret, it was time to take a huge gamble. The country desperately needed an election, but the only way to get one was to put down a motion of No Confidence, and win it. But the political parties in Parliament then were so finely balanced that no one could predict how such a vote would turn out. Would she chance it? She made her decision: it was a chance Britain had to have. The motion was tabled.

During the entire day of the vote, Westminster was in a fever of uncertainty. Colleagues kept rushing in with news of so-and-so changing his vote. Someone had been taken ill; another would not be able to get back because of the strikes. One Labour MP said he wanted a word with me, it was strictly private, but would I promise to give my Chief Whip a very confidential message to the effect that if we Tories promised to give him a peerage, he would vote with us. I delivered the message with as straight a face as I could muster, but the Chief almost fell off his bar stool with hilarity. That was one vote we did without. I might add that at this time, all the catering staff in Parliament were on strike. The bar staff were not. There was nothing to eat, but a very great deal to drink. A somewhat riotous atmosphere reigned.

At 10 p.m. precisely, we trooped out to vote. Not a soul knew how it would go. Back to our seats, there was not a spare inch in the public or press galleries, or, of course, in the Chamber itself. After what seemed like an interminable time, the count was over. We were transfixed. In came the Labour Deputy Chief Whip, grinning from ear to ear. I saw Margaret, sitting on the front bench, go as white as a sheet. Two minutes later, our own Deputy entered. He held up one *finger. We had won by one vote. The whole House erupted when Mr Speaker announced the result, and, with dignity, Mr Callaghan came to the despatch box to say that he would be handing in his resignation to Her Majesty in the morning.*

So Margaret Thatcher became Prime Minister, and set to work with a will.

And as she stepped down after eleven-and-a-half years as Britain's first and only woman Prime Minister, that final drama, too, was played out in the Chamber of the House of Commons, on the afternoon of 22 November

1990. We were all there. The Chamber was packed. The
atmosphere was extraordinary and highly emotional, with
everyone wondering if she would break down under the
sheer weight of the occasion, our feelings veering from
guilt to sympathy to admiration. Here was a woman who
had led Britain for the past eleven years, who had been
chucked out by her Cabinet and her party, and who still
had the raw guts to come into the Chamber for Prime
Minister's Questions and to answer a No Confidence
debate. Parliamentary occasions billed as epoch-making
often turn to anti-climax. This one did not.

Margaret Thatcher in *The Downing Street Years* gives her
own account of the occasion.

No one will ever understand British politics who does not
understand the House of Commons. The House is not just
another legislative body. On special occasions, it becomes
in some almost mystical way the focus of national feeling.
As newspaper comments and the reflections of those who
were present will testify, I was not alone in sensing the
concentrated emotion of that afternoon. And it seemed
as if this very intensity, mingled with the feelings of relief
that my great struggle against mounting odds had ended,
lent wings to my words ... The speech I rose to deliver does
not read in Hansard as a particularly eloquent one. It is a
fighting defence of the government's record ... which owes
more to the Conservative Research Department than to
Burke. For me at that moment, however, each sentence

was my testimony at the bar of History. It was as if I were speaking for the last time, rather than merely for the last time as Prime Minister.

Those are not the feelings of someone who saw herself as an outsider in Parliament, despite accusations from others that she was not clubbable and not a team player in the boys' public school atmosphere which still prevails in the Commons.

Her attitude to the conventions of Cabinet government was considerably more iconoclastic. Many historians have attributed her eventual loss of support within the Conservative Party to that very fact. There can be no doubt that in the end the Cabinet did for her: the worms finally turned. But she was very clear from the start that she was not interested in consensus government, even though her first Cabinets, as Michael Jopling points out in an earlier chapter, were a careful combination of supporters and opponents. It was not until 1983, after the Falklands and the Miners' Strike, that she felt able to surround herself with 'believers'.

In Peter Hennessy's *The Prime Minister*, Ian Gilmour defined it thus: 'Mrs Thatcher regarded her first Cabinet not as an aid to good government, but as an obstacle to be surmounted. Her belief that dialogue was a waste of time rather than a means of arriving at an agreed course of action was part of her rejection of consensus politics.'

But this, I think, was not simple bossiness. It came from her strongly held views about the role of a leader. In an

interview with Kenneth Harris while she was still Leader
of the Opposition, she said,

> If you choose a team in which you encounter a basic
> disagreement, you will not be able to carry out a
> programme, you won't be able to govern ... it must be a
> Cabinet that works on something much more than prag-
> matism or consensus. It must be a conviction government.

I served in the Cabinet of John Major. He famously said
that his predecessor had had the habit of announcing
the conclusions of a Cabinet at the start of the meeting.
One of his earliest decisions was to restore discussion and
debate to the Cabinet; this he most certainly did. There
was debate, there were votes, and majority decisions were
taken. He was determined to involve colleagues in collective responsibility, and he was right to do so. But of course,
colleagues lobbied one another for support on certain
decisions, private meetings took place before Cabinet and
ministers arrived briefed to the hilt by their departments;
there was all the usual political manoeuvring that might
be expected at the heart of the political process, so that,
inevitably, what might have seemed an open Cabinet decision had in fact been pre-determined, but by colleagues,
not by the Prime Minister.

Margaret Thatcher had had only one Cabinet job before
becoming opposition leader and then Prime Minister. She
had not in any sense trained up for the job and everything

about her personality suggests that she would expect her very closest political colleagues to be fellow travellers in all the causes they knew she stood for. Her management of Cabinet meetings in the early days of her premiership was, in fact, very orthodox. But after the Falklands War, the Miners' Strike and her election victory in 1983, her style became steadily more and more abrasive. Cabinet meetings became a one-woman band, and while some colleagues, like Nigel Lawson, welcomed them as an opportunity for quiet personal reflection, others chafed against her style and, on occasion, her rudeness.

Geoffrey Howe, in his autobiography, describes a Cabinet meeting on 21 June 1989 which discussed the War Crimes Bill. This had been defeated by a huge margin in the Lords, and the question was whether the Parliament Act should be used to force the will of the Commons on to the Lords to get the policy through. Geoffrey Howe believed that the government should accept its defeat in the Lords, not least on the grounds that the Bill would 'extend British jurisdiction, extraterritorially as well as retrospectively, and to do so for the sake of bringing proceedings, on the basis of evidence that was bound to be shaky because ancient, against defendants (i.e. Nazi war criminals) who were already in the twilight of their lives'. But Mrs Thatcher suddenly took a different view, possibly because

it was only two weeks since she had visited Babi Yar in Kiev, the memorial to the 30,000 Jews the Nazis had murdered there. She seemed to be particularly provoked, however, by the fact that it was the Lords who were standing in her way. That argument would not have carried such weight during our earlier years in office. Now however, Margaret discounted arguments, much heeded in the Lords, from champions of tradition and justice, such as Lords Shawcross, Home, Hailsham and Whitelaw. The last two were no longer in her Cabinet. How we missed their voices on an issue like this! Cabinet loyalty to principles which they felt instinctively seemed to have departed with them. The discussion concluded, predictably, in accordance with Margaret's wishes.

The War Crimes Bill received Royal Assent in May 1991.

Legends abound about the conduct of the Cabinet in the later years of Margaret Thatcher's premiership. I have been told more than once of colleagues who were physically sick the night before Cabinet if they had a difficult presentation to make. *Spitting Image*, the satirical political puppet show, showed appalling scenes of the Prime Minister shouting at her ministers, cowing them into silence and treating them with the utmost disdain. In earlier chapters of this book, John Major and Geoffrey Howe write about displays of rudeness in Cabinet from Margaret Thatcher. David Howell, a member of her Cabinet, is quoted by Peter Hennessy in *The Prime Minister*:

If by conviction government it is meant that certain slogans were going to be elevated and written in tablets of stone and used as the put-down at the end of every argument, then of course that is what happened ... Of course there is a deterring effect if one knows that one's going to go, not into a discussion where various points of view will be weighed and gradually a view may be achieved, but into a huge argument where tremendous battle lines will be drawn up and everyone who doesn't fall into line will be hit on the head.

You might have thought that ministers' special advisers would perhaps be exempt from the challenging treatment handed out to their masters, but it was not so.

Elizabeth Cottrell describes a meeting of special advisers in September 1987.

The Prime Minister began by suggesting that we advisers were an unnecessary extravagance. 'What use are you?' she asked. After a long silence one bold spirit ventured, 'You see, Prime Minister, we can say the ridiculous.' Her answer came, sharp as an arrow, 'I sincerely hope you don't.'

One by one, advisers and their departments' policies were shot down in flames. Little resistance was offered. Then it was my turn. I had just been appointed special adviser to Richard Luce, Minister for the Arts, then not even a Cabinet post. Mr Luce had put forward some very modest proposals to charge for certain library services. Mrs Thatcher, some thought surprisingly, was opposed to these. 'Tell your minister to stop this – he's quite mistaken, libraries should be free,' she declared.

I remembered that evening in 1982 and gathered up my courage. 'You are wrong, Prime Minister,' I replied. There was a moment of appalled silence, while my colleagues waited in fearful glee for my annihilation. But she asked, in a perfectly measured tone, 'Why, Elizabeth?' and I tried to explain. I'm not sure if I converted her, but she listened intently and acknowledged that some of my arguments held water. After all, it is difficult to be terrified of someone who had run you a bath at three o'clock in the morning.

Keith Simpson, MP for Broadland, was, before he was elected to the Commons in 1997, Special Adviser to George Younger, Secretary of State for Defence. He describes a meeting for special advisers held a year after Elizabeth Cottrell's.

In July 1988, John Whittingdale, Margaret Thatcher's political secretary, wrote to all special advisers inviting them to a meeting with her in Downing Street on 3 October just before the Party Conference. In John's words, it was 'a three-line whip with no bisques'. The previous meeting between Margaret Thatcher and the special advisers had been a year before [described above by Elizabeth Cottrell], and when I asked them what it was like, it became apparent that it was something that filled them with both apprehension – because she really grilled them over policy – and expectation – because it was a privilege to have such an opportunity with a very busy Prime Minister.

I took advice from Andrew Dunlop, my predecessor at the MoD, and then in the Policy Unit, and Archie Hamilton, who had been her PPS and was now Minister of State for the Armed Forces. Both emphasised that you had to be on top of your brief, to expect to be interrupted and challenged and under no circumstances to be over-whelmed by her questions and sheer verbal firepower.

The civil servants in George Younger's private office were filled with foreboding. I was told that while she admired the armed forces and placed a high priority on defence of the realm, she believed the MoD was profligate, incompetent and hopeless at procuring weapons and equipment. I was told that on my shoulders rested the reputation of my Secretary of State, the MoD and, not least, my own future. Gulp!

Classically, George Younger was relatively relaxed about the meeting and said he assumed I would be well briefed and would know how to deal with her – 'Good luck.'

I knew that the Prime Minister would quiz me about defence budget overruns and the cost of new weapons, including a replacement main battle tank for the army, where the choice was between the German Leopard, the American Abrams and the British Challenger. I had read a note by Charles Powell from her private office about when recently she had met the chairman of Vickers, who were lobbying for Challenger. She told him she was fed up buying British equipment that didn't work. He replied that his tanks were made under warranty. Magisterially, Margaret Thatcher replied, 'It is no good the British Army going to war with tanks under warranty!'

Cometh the day, cometh the trial. Late on the afternoon of 3 October, all the advisers, about a dozen of us, gathered in the Cabinet Room with John Whittingdale and Robin Harris, Director of the Conservative Research Department. Charles Powell hovered in the wings. The Prime Minister came in, and my immediate reaction was to think she looked tired, frail and somewhat bowed. She fiddled with her necklace and the neck of her jacket all the time. But any first impression of frailty and tiredness was soon swept away as the meeting began. She told us that she wanted to hear what we were putting into our ministers' speeches for the Party Conference, what were the main issues in our departments, and looking for ideas for the future. She emphasised the need to control public expenditure and emphasised the role of the individual as against the state. She was quite pessimistic about public borrowing and credit, and, in a swipe at the Treasury, said if we were a Labour government, critics would have a field day.

Then the inquisition began as she went round the table questioning adviser after adviser about ministerial plans and policies. I was fascinated to observe how my colleagues dealt with her aggressive line of questions and continual interruptions. The Treasury advisers were over-confident and rather arrogant initially, but soon retired hurt. Despite their valiant efforts, the advisers at Transport, Health and Social Security were brushed aside. Patrick Rock at Environment and Anthony Teasdale at the FCO argued their corner and were not overwhelmed by her questioning. The Cabinet table began to resemble a casualty clearing station.

Finally she came to me and said, 'You are Keith Simpson at Defence, what have you got to say for yourself?' Perhaps with more bravura than common sense, I replied, like Oliver Twist, 'We'd like some more money.' There was a split second of total silence, then the Prime Minister, in that well-known raised voice said, 'More money!' For about two minutes, although it appeared longer, she worked herself up to a splendid fury, and, without pausing for breath, launched a violent attack on the MoD and all its failing – extravagant budgets, overspends, procurement failures. Out of the corner of my eye I could see my fellow advisers looking either very apprehensive at me having raised a whirlwind or gleeful that I was the object of so much focused fury. It was impossible to get a word in edgeways, and later I said to my wife, Pepi, that I'd learned in our marriage to let exhaustion come into play and then attempt to explain my case. Briefly I was able to point out that government policy was strong defence, she had agreed on new equipment, including a replacement tank, and that the MoD under George Younger, who had replaced Michael Heseltine – at that point a startling glint appeared in her eye – was getting to grips with MoD failures. She merely nodded and passed on to the next adviser. The meeting ended with neither tea nor a proper drink.

I left thinking that I had been well and truly chewed over. But at the door the Prime Minister stopped me and, to my surprise, said I had argued my case very well and that she valued robust debate.

It took about ten minutes to get back to the ministerial floor in the MoD opposite Downing Street. I was greeted by members of the private office wailing and tearing their clothes, saying how could I have got into an argument with the Prime Minister, what was I thinking of, the reputation of the MoD was irreparably damaged, I could expect an interview with George Younger when he heard what I had said. It was fascinating to think that all over Whitehall, private offices had been in contact with No. 10 to find out what had happened at the advisers' meeting.

Later I told George Younger the gist of the meeting and he roared with laughter, saying it was a good learning experience, and now I realised what Cabinet ministers went through. Looking back on the meeting, I thought what a formidable and remarkable Prime Minister she was, who after nearly ten years had command over so much policy and had clear, if at times rigid, objectives and prejudices. Certainly I had learned a lesson about 'going over the top' in the face of such a formidable politician. Perhaps I should have followed the example of Peter Luff, the DTI adviser, who had managed to hide behind others so that Margaret Thatcher could not see him and was thus never questioned. His minister, David Young, congratulated him on this achievement!

One of the most telling points in Keith Simpson's account is the reaction of his Secretary of State, George Younger, explaining that he had undergone an experience very familiar to every Cabinet minister. There is no excuse for rude or bullying tactics, of course, although they are commonplace in my experience, not only in political life, but also in boardrooms, at university high tables and in every profession. But there is too much evidence to ignore that Mrs Thatcher did become increasingly overbearing in her approach, particularly in the second half of her premiership. It is also the case that you cannot get the best out of colleagues with such an approach. In the end, the worms turned. The outsider was herself ejected.

As far as Margaret Thatcher's doctrine of Us and Them was concerned, the civil service and its works were definitely Them. Her attitude, formed at the Ministry of Pensions and National Insurance where she was a junior minister, and at the Department of Education and Science where she held her first Cabinet post, never altered, although she had real respect and indeed affection for a number of individual officials.

It is at least possible that the condescending attitudes she met from senior officials in her first ministerial posts influenced her later attitude. In Hugo Young's *One of Us*, the Permanent Secretary, Sir Eric Bowyer, was apparently concerned, when she arrived at the Ministry of Pensions, that her family responsibilities, with her two young children and a husband, would hamper her ability to put in the hours necessary. He was further concerned that her immaculate appearance meant that she spent hours at the hairdresser's and the dressmaker's. He need not have worried, since her home life was efficiently organised, and with her addiction to heated rollers and skill with a needle, she was well able to take care of her own grooming. In the end, he was forced to concede that she worked as hard as anyone and harder than many. But she may well have asked herself if he would have had the same anxieties about a new young male minister.

It was the same at the Department of Education and Science, where Sir William Pile, the Permanent Secretary, was struck by her obvious distrust of the civil service and her determination from the moment of her arrival to put her stamp on policy and to get very prompt action from the Department – apparently a new experience for Sir William and his colleagues. I am led to wonder what her predecessors thought their roles were.

I have a lot of sympathy for Margaret Thatcher's attitude. I found in my encounters with civil servants some of the most dedicated and knowledgeable people imaginable in any profession. But I also found loftiness worthy of any episode of *Yes, Minister*. On my first morning as Minister of State at the Treasury, in December 1990, I was visited by the Permanent Secretary, the very grand Sir Peter Middleton. He said, 'I think you should know at once that in the Treasury, junior ministers are of no account. Our work is done with the Chancellor. For your information, the Treasury does not introduce measures with 38 million losers, like the poll tax, and by the way, there is no lavatory for women ministers, as you are the first we have had.' I howled with silent laughter for weeks.

Margaret Thatcher believed that to govern was to act. Action and results were what mattered, and process, of which obviously the civil service was not only the master, but also an essential part, was of no interest to her. Ian Beesley in an earlier chapter of this book recalls a seminar for junior ministers in 1985, where Margaret Thatcher declared, 'You have been appointed to get results, not just to hold office.' She confirms this in *The Path to Power*, where she writes of detecting in the Department of Education and Science 'opposition between my own executive style of decision-making and the more consultative style to which [the officials] were accustomed'. Worse, she also detected a self-righteously socialist ethos. In short, 'It was soon clear to me that on the whole I was not among friends.'

Later on, she came to regard some of the most senior

civil servants who worked with her at No. 10 as her most trusted friends and colleagues.

Robert Armstrong, as Secretary of the Cabinet, certainly fell into that category. He recalls two occasions on which she agreed reforms to the civil service and which illustrate superbly how a good relationship between an elected politician, even a potentially hostile one, and a skilled official can achieve smooth change.

In the autumn of 1981, the Prime Minister decided, after taking advice from Sir Derek Rayner (her adviser on efficiency in government) to abolish the Civil Service Department and to divide its functions between the Treasury and the Cabinet office, which took responsibility for organisational, welfare and conduct and disciplinary issues. The Permanent Secretary of the Civil Service Department took early retirement and it was necessary to appoint a successor to him as Head of the Home Civil Service. The Prime Minister accepted by recommendation that the Permanent Secretary to the Treasury, Sir Douglas Wass, and I should be joint heads, but when Douglas Wass retired eighteen months later, she decided that his successor should not be appointed Joint Head of the Civil Service. 'I don't want to go on with a Pinky-and-Perky arrangement, Robert, you'll have to do it on your own.' As I thought (and still think) that it is right that the Secretary of the Cabinet should be the Head of the Home Civil Service, I did not demur.

Towards the end of my term of office I thought the time had come for the issue of a memorandum of guidance on the duties of civil servants in relation to ministers. I prepared a draft and discussed it with my fellow Permanent Secretaries. When I had a final draft, I sent it to the Prime Minister, who was the Minister of the Civil Service, explaining that I proposed to issue it on my own authority as Head of the Home Civil Service and was not asking for her to give it her formal approval, but that I wanted her to be aware of it and I hoped that she would lay it before Parliament as an annex to a Written Parliamentary Question. She was entirely content with this arrangement.

Nor did Margaret Thatcher's general antipathy blind her to the rights of public servants. Ian Beesley writes,

Even on an issue on which she was determined, such as banning trade union membership at the Government Communications Head Quarters (GCHQ), I recall her reflecting aloud that people were being asked to give up a right and should be compensated for doing so – causing a very senior figure to comment that he had heard the shops in Cheltenham were currently buoyant. Thatcher dropped her head to look into her lap, and only came up smiling when the rest of the attendees laughed. She did not readily get a joke.

Despite these benign examples, however, she remained until the end of her premiership defiantly of the view that the whole of the civil service, the professions, local government and indeed most of the Establishment got in the way of the legitimately elected government.

Indeed, on occasion, she felt she had to take the side of the people against the government. Stephen Sherbourne, her political secretary, would on occasion hear her with

Denis, talking about 'the government' as if she were nothing to do with it. She was always delighted to find a source of information which contradicted the advice she was being given from an official channel. As John Wakeham said in an earlier chapter, 'I very soon learned that if she took a letter out of her handbag, it was not just important, it contained views she instinctively felt were right.'

Ian Beesley agrees:

We organised an 'eye-catching demonstration' of the scale and burden of government forms, with the help of the Plain English Campaign and its joint leader, Chrissie Maher. An exhibition of forms was staged in the central lobby of the Palace of Westminster, and the Plain English people had brought two elderly ladies from Salford to bring alive the problems some people had in filling in the forms for benefits. The two were sat on upright chairs and went to stand when the Prime Minister approached them. She insisted they sit back down, and then knelt to hear their story and to have it repeated directly to Norman Fowler, who was then Secretary of State for Social Security. The empathy was clear. Government was failing those and others like them because the bureaucratic processes were too cumbersome, the forms they had to complete were too unintelligible and the individuals too proud to admit defeat.

As far as her relations with the newspapers were concerned, Margaret Thatcher had what I once heard described as the simple policy of not reading them, knighting their editors and ennobling their proprietors. Michael Brunson, the distinguished ITN political commentator, writes:

In her dealings with the media, Mrs T. employed the same brisk efficiency that she brought to government. Not for her what one later Downing Street Press Secretary called 'the daily necessity of throwing chunks of red meat to the press pack in order to satisfy their insatiable appetite for news'. By and large, she talked to us only when she had something important to say. Occasionally she would chat for a few minutes after a one-to-one interview and let slip a remark which could perhaps be used as deep background – once telling me, for example, that all the House of Commons really did was to hold up what she wanted to achieve for a year, or when a colleague learned that she was planning an inflation target of 3 per cent – something which she had not previously vouchsafed to her Chancellor of the Exchequer.

Peter Riddell writes:

Margaret Thatcher did not have much time for working political journalists, like those of us who ran political teams in the Press Gallery. She regarded us as a mixture of the ill-informed, the ill-intentioned and the ill-directed. Journalism was not really a proper job. She would never use a term like 'reptiles' about us as her beloved husband, Denis, did. But there was a similar feeling of detachment and contempt.

Her preferred media contacts were with proprietors and ideologically sympathetic editors and columnists, those who were 'one of us'. This was in marked contrast with some of her predecessors, like Harold Wilson, and all her successors, who, at least during their rise to the top and in their early years as Prime Minister, cultivated friendly relations with political editors and correspondents, using first names at press conferences.

For Mrs Thatcher it was always Mr Riddell, never Peter. And in many ways, quite right too. I have never called a serving Prime Minister by their first name, however well I knew them beforehand, and however friendly our relations afterwards. Mrs Thatcher created a certain mystique out of distance. There was always a little danger about her, apprehension of a damning put-down or memorable eruption.

Bernard Ingham was her faithful emissary to us, with his bluff Yorkshire bark, and occasional bite. He was his mistress's voice, intuitively understanding her instincts and moods, even if often anticipating rather than directly reporting on them. Bernard was always the loyal retainer below stairs, not a confidant sharing her late-night thoughts in the flat over a glass of whisky. He was an interpreter, and a very good one. He was not himself a player, unlike, say, Alastair Campbell during the Blair years. Bernard was there to handle the media on her behalf so that she would not have to do so.

Her fierce antagonism towards the Establishment and all its works marked much of her domestic policy. The professions, the City, the academic world, the civil service, the press – all of them came into her sights. She was too much of a career politician to extend that antipathy to the House of Commons. But in the end, she was not in power for those who started with advantage on their side, but for the kind of working people she had grown up with in Grantham. And they rewarded her for that with their votes in three successive general elections.

NINE

'WITH DENIS THERE I WAS NEVER ALONE. WHAT A MAN. WHAT A HUSBAND. WHAT A FRIEND.'

Margaret Thatcher prided herself on being an outsider. She chose to marry, in Denis, a man who could hardly have been more of an insider. No one could have been more clubbable than he was. A keen sportsman and golfer with a real skill for affable small talk, he had a knack for putting others at their ease if he felt they were uncomfortable in any way. His clear and consistent views, which chimed with those of the *Telegraph*, were supportive of his wife and impatient of her critics. His hail-fellow-well-met manner successfully concealed his knowledgeable and successful business acumen, his wicked sense of humour and his ability to send himself up. Ever present at dinners, functions and conferences, often heard muttering 'leftie', 'nonsense' and so on, there was the Prime Minister's husband. He was in many ways her mainstay, and he really did resemble the caricature of himself so memorably portrayed in the famous 'Dear Bill' letters in *Private Eye*.

The contributors to this book have been sparing in their mentions of Denis, although such mentions as there are, are appreciative of his role and character. I can recall meeting Denis only once. I had been invited with my husband to lunch at Chequers early on in my very junior ministerial career. We were both rather dreading it, not knowing quite what to expect, but, when we arrived, Denis picked out Tom as the other non-political person in the room and whisked him away to have an excellent and long chat about sit-on lawn mowers, which they both greatly enjoyed.

Denis was almost as popular as his wife in her constituency of Finchley. Harvey Thomas writes that Mrs Thatcher regarded Finchley as 'her real foundation' and adds: 'The marvellous Denis felt the same way! They both knew whatever political issues and battles she had to face as Prime Minister, the friends in Finchley were always there, ready to encourage her at any hour.' As of course was Denis.

Sir Richard Parsons, the former ambassador, is the one exception among the contributors to this book to provide an account devoted solely to Denis. It describes a hilarious conversation between him and the wife of the Spanish Prime Minister. The occasion was the visit of the Spanish Prime Minister to Downing Street for the signing of an agreement between Spain and Britain on the relaxation of access between Spain and Gibraltar.

The Spanish delegation appeared and agreement was soon reached. Lunch followed. The two Prime Ministers were at the first table with the two foreign ministers. I was placed at the second one, with Mrs Calvo-Sotelo, wife of the Spanish Prime Minister, and Denis Thatcher. Denis Thatcher tried to present himself in public as a jovial idiot but I could see at once that he was no such thing. He started by giving a parody of the weird figure he liked to present.

'I have been to Spain several times,' he began heartily. 'One of my favourite spots for the hols. Good cheap booze and quick service when you clap your hands. Jolly good golf too!' He enthused for some time about the material pleasures of the warm south. Special emphasis was laid on the cheap booze. I was to transmit all this nonsense to dignified Mrs Calvo-Sotelo.

'Mr Thatcher is saying how much he admires the civilisation of your beautiful country,' I told her in my best Spanish. 'Your great history, your devotion to the Christian faith, the work of your brave missionaries in South America and your wonderful religious paintings,' I droned on, as Denis Thatcher recalled with gusto how cheap the cigars were on the Costa del Sol.

'Do go on,' murmured Mrs Calvo-Sotelo in Spanish. I realised that she spoke English almost perfectly. It was a happy occasion. I saw then that Mrs T. was lucky in her mate.

And so she was, and even luckier that she knew it.

TEN

'WOMEN SHOULD AIM HIGH, IN POLITICS NOT LEAST.'

So wrote Margaret Thatcher in the *Sunday Graphic* in 1952, on the accession to the throne of the young Queen Elizabeth II. She added, 'Why not a woman Chancellor, a woman Foreign Secretary?'

Most of her biographers, and, in particular, feminist commentators, point out that although in 1952, before she started on her own parliamentary career, the young Margaret Thatcher apparently believed that there was no limit to women's potential, she did nothing to help them fulfil that potential once she herself had reached the top.

It is indisputable that Margaret Thatcher did not promote women into her Cabinet. Although she made Janet Young Leader of the House of Lords, the first woman to hold that post, and in that capacity Lady Young attended Cabinet from 1981 to 1983, people were quick to point out that it did not really count, because it was a House of Lords position. It was a different matter in the Commons. She appointed a number of able women to ministerial posts; some, like Lynda Chalker and Angela Rumbold, reached the position of Minister of State, but she promoted them no further. She encouraged her junior women ministers and took notice of what they said. The same went for Conservative women MPs, who saw her regularly and lobbied her on concerns particular to women, especially on the regular occasions when it seemed that the Treasury might have its eyes on an issue especially relevant to women, for example child benefit. She was close to senior women in the Conservative Party, as Joan Seccombe later explains. She was very conscious of the women's vote, and from the very beginning of her political career, quite shamelessly appealed to women voters by being prepared to be interviewed about clothes and domestic matters. She constantly explained policy matters by using household examples: the housewife needing to balance her budget, for example. But the fact that she did not bring other women into the Cabinet cannot be ignored.

It is also indisputable that she failed other feminist tests. She did not take up the cause of reducing unequal treatment for women in the workplace, although she could have done; she had, after all, always worked herself. Given her strong belief in self-help, she might well have made much of the need to engage in public life the 52 per cent of the population accounted for by women. She could have encouraged more women to come into politics, although she did support Emma Nicholson's High Flyers initiative in the early 1980s which had that aim, and was indeed very successful.

I believe that there are a number of reasons for her lack of interest, apparent or real. One reason may well be – and many have advanced this argument – that she was a queen bee and wanted no competition in the hive. But as always with Margaret Thatcher, there are no facile explanations, and the truth about her is always complicated.

Chapter 8 of this book explored the various ways in which Margaret Thatcher was an outsider in the world she chose to conquer. We have seen how she described herself as being 'portrayed as an outsider, who, by some odd mixture of circumstances had stepped inside and stayed there for eleven-and-a-half years; in my case the portrayal was not inaccurate'. If she felt herself to be an outsider by class, education, academic discipline and formation, how much more of an outsider, in the world she had chosen, did she feel herself to be as a woman? And not just any woman, but the first woman to be Prime Minister of Britain?

There is no indication that her father, the formidable Alderman Roberts, saw any particular limit to what she could achieve. There is no record of him telling her that she could not do this or that because she was a woman. She went to a girls' school and a women's college at Oxford, and did not lack for female role models. The thought that she might be prevented by her gender from doing what she wanted does not seem to have occurred to her. She apparently had no difficulty in getting a job as a research scientist, qualifying for the Bar and entering Chambers, although she does say in *The Path to Power* that she was, as a woman, at times made to 'feel small in industry, at the Bar, and in Tory constituency politics'. She did have misgivings about becoming an MP when the pay would not have been enough to support her, but once the job attracted a salary of a thousand pounds per annum, she knew she could afford to pursue her aim. In the event, of course, she married a rich man, and, as she always pointed out, this helped in many ways, not least with the cost of childcare and secretarial help in the Commons. It really is possible that she thought that other women could do what she had done.

It is also possible to argue that her generation – she was born in 1925 – had something to do with her apparent imperviousness to the enormous wave of feminist thought which hit Britain in the early 1960s, with much media coverage and discussion of the ideas of Betty Friedan and Simone de Beauvoir. Until she set out on her political career, she had encountered no insuperable problems on account of her gender. She was already a noticeable and ambitious MP by the time that women everywhere were talking about feminism. She would certainly not have wished to be typecast as an MP over-concerned with 'women's issues', and it is at least possible that she deliberately concentrated on other policy areas, like the economy. It is entirely understandable that she might not have wanted to become pigeon-holed. The sheer amount of prejudice she encountered on her way to the top might have felled a lesser mortal. To have courted even more prejudice and snubs for devoting herself to causes important mainly to women would have been too much to expect from any politician of her generation determined to reach the top.

When she arrived in the Commons, it was to encounter an atmosphere of comfortable clubby male exclusiveness, where women were an oddity and emphatically not One of Us. She apparently felt that ability was valued regardless of gender among MPs, but her view does not seem have been shared by many of her male colleagues. There were only twelve women Conservative MPs, including her, and as Jim Prior put it, 'The few women in the parliamentary party tended not to be accepted so easily by their male colleagues' (Campbell, *Margaret Thatcher*, p.123).

(Old House of Commons habits die quite hard. When I arrived there in 1987, thirty years later, one senior Conservative colleague called me Betty. When I corrected him, he said, 'Oh, I call you all Betty, you all look the same to me.')

According to Brenda Maddox, when Margaret Thatcher first entered the Commons she was not regarded as particularly clubbable even by other women MPs. But she did understand the importance of women in Parliament working together in a common cause, which was, as she confided to Shirley Williams: 'We have to show them (the men) that we're better than they are.' Shirley Williams added that she got the impression that Mrs Thatcher found men 'agreeable, playful, and in the end not very serious creatures'.

If women were a rare breed as backbenchers, they were even rarer in government. There are countless examples in this book of the condescension and disdain with which Margaret Thatcher was treated, as a minister and Secretary of State, and as Leader of the Opposition, simply because she was a woman. Some civil service mandarins were as patronising as her political colleagues. Both in the country and within the Conservative Party, there was a broad body of opinion that doubted her ability, as a woman, to lead the party to victory in the 1979 election, and, when she had done that, to be a credible Prime Minister.

Interestingly, this perception was never shared by the so-called blue-collar voters in the C1 and C2 categories, or to put it another way, the skilled working class, who consistently supported her throughout her premiership. I will always remember, in 1987, canvassing around 300 or so women agricultural workers, or gang women, during their lunch break in a horticultural nursery. These women were as tough as it gets, on a par with the famous 'buffies' in the Sheffield steel industry, or those sorting coal at the drift mines of Cumbria. I asked which way they were going to vote in the election. They said, 'For Mrs Thatcher.' I asked why. They replied, 'Because she tell the men.'

But one should not underestimate the degree of disbelief

and anxiety from others that surrounded her as a woman leader who held the party's fortunes in her hand. After her first speech as leader at the Conservative Party Conference in 1975, Denis Thatcher confessed that he had not been so frightened of anything since the war, such was the apprehension about the reaction of the party faithful to a woman leader. The speech got a warm welcome, in the event, but that welcome was by no means guaranteed beforehand.

Even when she became Prime Minister, the sniping from male colleagues did not stop. Sir Richard Parsons gives a truly dreadful example of Cabinet disloyalty in the early 1980s. He begins by describing his first meeting with Margaret Thatcher at a meeting of the European Security Conference in Budapest, in 1977.

I had long been interested in Mrs Thatcher, a graduate of Somerville College, Oxford, like my mother. For all her external toughness, it was obvious from the start that Margaret Thatcher was really rather a kind woman brimming with feminine virtues. To my surprise, I found that I was not afraid of her at all. That was a great relief. I started by telling her that my mother, like her, had been at Somerville, though many years before. I said that at the end of her life, she had said how glad she was that a Somerville woman would one day become Prime Minister, though it was a pity, she thought, 'that she only read stinks'. That was an old-fashioned slang word for chemistry. Mrs T. responded with a cold glance. But she must have been amused because I later heard her repeating my story on the other side of the room.

Between 1980 and 1984, Sir Richard served as Britain's ambassador in Madrid.

Spain had been out of bounds to most British politicians during the Franco era. They did not want to appear to be hobnobbing with the last of the Fascist dictators. Now they seized the opportunity to remedy this deficiency. About half of the Thatcher Cabinet came to stay with me in Madrid. Over late-night drinks, they told me how things were going at home. I was almost shocked to find that with the notable exception of loyal deputies such as Willie Whitelaw and Peter Carrington, most of the Thatcher ministers had in private a distinctly satirical attitude towards their own Prime Minister. They even gave imitations of the great lady. And they talked about her in a way that no British Cabinet minister would have spoken about a male Prime Minister. It was clear that Mrs T. was paying the price for being our first woman Prime Minister. Take, for example, her amiable habit of breaking off long meetings at No. 10 to go upstairs and personally brew tea and coffee for all concerned. They seemed to see this as a hilarious womanly peculiarity. I just thought how human she seemed to be. My suspicion is that this sort of attitude put pressure on Mrs T. to toughen up and become more strident and demanding as her long term of office increased the strain. She did, after all, have to deal with such adversaries as the Argentine colonels and the aggressive leaders of the unfortunate miners.

Sir Richard might have added, 'and also those she might legitimately have assumed to be on her side'.

One could therefore argue that a woman politician who

had endured all of this would be very cautious in what and how much she said about the cause of women, for the sake of her own credibility, not to say survival, in the context of the 1970s and 1980s. Given the nature of the particu-lar challenges she had to face – extraordinary economic problems, the Falklands conflict, the Miners' Strike, and European issues – she might perhaps be forgiven for not giving the advancement of women more prominence, or, if not forgiven, at least understood.

One of the best records that exists of Margaret Thatcher's own views on the subject of women is contained in the lecture she gave in late July 1982 to the Society of Townswomen's Guilds, reproduced in full in the Appendix. The lecture was in celebration of the centenary of Dame Margery Corbett Ashby, the distinguished campaigner for women's rights.

She points out in the lecture that at that time, 1982, there were only twenty-one women MPs in a House of Commons with 635 members in all, a fact she thinks would have disappointed the early suffragettes. She says that, following in the tradition of Asquith and Gladstone, who opposed women's suffrage,

Winston Churchill had often felt the same way about women in political life. And when I went to see Lady Churchill, shortly after I became Leader of the Party – because I wanted to see her, she was a wonderful woman in her own right – and she reminded me of this; and she said, 'but you know I always used to argue with Winston over it'.

And I guess she did.

She asserts that while her generation takes the view that 'the home should be the centre but not the boundary of a woman's life', women bring 'special talents and experiences to public life', precisely because they 'bear the children and run the home'. This is a view she often repeated, emphasising that women are the doers in public life, while men are the talkers. (It is also a view frequently advanced by today's prominent women; they call it multi-tasking.)

She also claims that

> the battle for women's rights has been largely won. The days when these were demanded and discussed in strident tones should be gone for ever. And I hope they are. I hated those strident tones that you still hear from some Women's Libbers. The battle is largely won, but we must now see women's rights in perspective and turn our attention to how we could use human rights to build the kind of world we wish our children to live in.

The content of this lecture is drafted with the utmost care, to balance her view that women could and should achieve as she had, with her equally strong view that women's domestic role brought particular insights and skills into the workplace.

Just two weeks after she left office she gave an interview

to Fiona Millar for *The House* magazine (an incredible demonstration of courage in itself), in which she talked about Denis and the family, and about combining her work as an MP with her family responsibilities.

I was very lucky because my husband worked in town, we lived in town and most of my work was here (in the Commons). It would have been very different had Denis worked in Leeds or Manchester or Glasgow. I couldn't have done half the things I have done. He has been a tremendously important part of my life and we were never far away from the children. When they went to boarding schools we deliberately chose ones which were close at hand so we could always get there very quickly. I didn't stand in the 1955 election because the children were too young, and then Finchley came along about 1958 and I applied and got it. I could only have applied for seats which were close to London. I just didn't feel I could leave the children ... The other great thing about being an MP is that some of the holidays coincide with the children's, so I was able to spend some time with them then. Although I was very busy and out and about, I could take them around with me so it fitted in very well.

I think you could just as easily say that the Westminster system isn't geared for men as for women. You do have to sacrifice a great deal but it has worked very well for most people ... there are a lot of jobs which involve travel, so I think sometimes you just have to make the very best of what you've got. Then life is brighter than if you are constantly looking at what you haven't got.

It is interesting that in this interview, she gives no hint at all that there should be special arrangements for women MPs, or indeed for any working women. She continued to insist on an even-handed approach to the interests of men and women. Conservative Party policy continues to oppose positive discrimination for women, a policy most visible in the party's continuing opposition to all-women shortlists for selecting parliamentary candidates.

However, Margaret Thatcher did have concerns about some policy areas which were obviously important to women. She frequently used the Conservative Women's National Committee as a sounding board, as Joan Seccombe remembers.

My first encounter with Margaret Thatcher was in the late 1960s when, as a new women's branch chairman in Yardley in Birmingham, I attended the Conservative National Conference in London. Margaret was one of the speakers and I have a vivid memory of her in a large blue hat with the brim bobbing up and down as she made her points. I did not see that hat again but, fortunately, it would be the first of many encounters I had with Margaret in the years to come.

In those days around 1,000 representatives attended the Conservative Women's Conference each year. Many of these women did not have outside careers and the income which went with this. Money was tight for young families and the branch secretaries used to collect a weekly amount from all representatives to ensure everyone had the funds to cover the expenses of the bus. The nation was still living through the aftermath of the war and these trips to London were the highlight of a much simpler life than the one we have today.

People were often more involved in the party at a variety of levels and membership levels were at a record high. The Conservative Party had 3 million members at this time. Membership of the party did not just satisfy political interests but allowed people to engage in the full range of social activities which were available. You were able to join the Young Conservatives and then work your way up through either the women's organisation or the Conservative Policy Centre, and all at a branch level. I worked my way up and was delighted when I reached my position as Women's Branch Chairman for the Acocks Green ward in the Yardley constituency. This enabled me to travel to the Women's Conference and see the range of speakers.

Margaret was young, glamorous and very articulate with the valuable asset of always being able to express herself in a simple manner which could be easily understood. We felt her to be one of us, the mother of small children who understood the difficulties of juggling life. We applauded her appointment as Secretary of State for Education in 1970, from where she started on her dazzling parliamentary career.

I came to know Margaret on a personal level when I was made an area women's chairman in 1977 and started attending biannual visits to No. 10. These meetings were an opportunity to discuss research papers which we had written on issues such as 'The Cinderella Service' – a paper highlighting the poor standing and pay nurses were given in the NHS at the time. This particular research paper was instigated by Lady Young and was a landmark for nurses in the NHS.

It was widely discussed by the public and in the media and thankfully helped change the position nurses were given in our society.

These meetings were not just social visits but provided a forum for serious political work and reporting to which the Prime Minister responded. We, in turn, were able to take back news and updates to the constituencies on the local issues they had raised. This clear conduit into the heart of government worked extremely well and showed an admirable engagement between No. 10 and the grass roots.

People often say that Margaret Thatcher was not a 'woman's woman', yet she always told us that she valued our comments more than most because she heard exactly what was happening on the ground in the constituencies. She heard it in a 'no holds barred' manner and encouraged us to be frank and open. We formed a group of well-briefed, feisty and fearless women and her welcome to us was warm and generous. I always felt that she gave the impression she had limitless time for us and our opinions.

I found as a new MP, and then as a very junior social security minister while Margaret Thatcher was Prime Minister, that there were certain policy areas on which she was immoveable, because they mattered to women. Child benefit was a case in point. Every year, Treasury ministers (or more probably Treasury officials) try to have a go at reducing the cost of universal child benefit. They certainly tried it on in preparations for the two Budgets when I was in the Treasury, in 1991 and 1992. It was undoubtedly the same with Margaret Thatcher at No. 10. She would say, time after time, 'This is the only payment which goes direct to the mother. It is hers for her children, and it must not be touched.'

In *The Downing Street Years* she writes about family policies:

There are limits beyond which 'family policy' should not seek to go. That is why I considered it important to encourage voluntary bodies which had the right values and vision, like Mrs Margaret Harrison's 'Homestart', whose 6,000 voluntary workers were themselves parents and offered friendship, common-sense advice, and support in the family home. I preferred if at all possible that direct help should come from someone other than professional social workers.

I was also appalled by the way in which men fathered a child and then absconded, leaving the single mother – and the taxpayer – to foot the bill for their irresponsibility and condemning the child to a lower standard of living. I thought it scandalous that only one in three children entitled to receive maintenance actually benefited from regular payments. So – against considerable opposition from Tony Newton, the Social Security Secretary, and from the Lord Chancellor's department – I insisted that a new Child Support Agency be set up, and that maintenance be based not just on the cost of bringing up a child but on that child's right to share in its parents' rising living standards. This was the background to the Child Support Act 1991.

I have a very clear memory of how her interest in a possible child support policy was aroused. I was answering Social

Security Questions in the Commons, as departmental
teams of ministers have to do monthly, fairly soon after I
had joined the Department in July 1989. One of my questions was on the subject of child support in the event of
a mother being abandoned by the father of her child. I
answered that a group of officials from the Department
were currently in Australia looking at the arrangements
there which required absent fathers to pay maintenance. I
added that we would be looking with interest at their findings, as we were concerned about the plight of mothers
and children in this situation. The *Evening Standard* reported
my answer that evening, and No. 10 came straight on the
phone to the Department. I was immediately summoned
to be dressed down by Tony Newton, the Secretary of
State. How dare I make policy at the despatch box? What
did I think I was doing? Why would the Prime Minister be
interested in anything I said, as the most junior minister in
the Department? And so on and so on. Tony Newton was
the most mild-mannered and kindly man imaginable, but
he was clearly terribly rattled. I weakly pointed out that I
had been following the official departmental brief in my
answer, but by this time he was beyond listening.

What followed was truly dramatic. He in his turn was
summoned to No. 10 and told that Mrs T. wanted to pursue
the policy. He was as knowledgeable as any official about all
aspects of social security policy, and he could see that a morass
of difficulties could attend the implementation of such a
scheme. Moreover, the Lord Chancellor, Lord Mackay, had

principled objections to maintenance arrangements being made outside a court of law. When Mrs Thatcher writes of opposition from Tony Newton and the Lord Chancellor she understates their views, but the legislation went ahead. History has proved that maybe they had a point.

While she appeared to be reluctant to accept that there were still real injustices for women in the workplace, in the City and in the professions, in which government might have intervened, she had no scruples about using her own gender to the utmost, for personal publicity as an MP and to give the best possible presentation of her case as party leader. She was not a vain woman, but she had at least two major makeovers during her career in order to look her best at all times. She considered it part of the job, but I believe she also enjoyed it.

Michael Jopling, her first Chief Whip when she became Prime Minister, writes,

I first met Margaret Thatcher soon after my election to the Commons in 1964. During the years of opposition until the Heath victory in 1970, I did not come to know her very well. But I recall being surprised and disappointed that such a good-looking woman dressed in a way that did not do her justice. I do not mean miniskirts, which many younger women wore; but the 1960s were a time of snappy dressing generally. When she did become Prime Minister her dress sense became much smarter and more elegant. Although the statue of her in the Members' Lobby at Westminster is meant to be in her later years, the poorly sculptured suit reflects the earlier days.

Soon after she became Leader of the Conservative Party, she met Gordon Reece, a television producer, and with his advice set about changing her image. He advised her on the best outfits to wear for television appearances, and to abandon her hats (although she insisted on continuing to wear her pearls, a gift from Denis after the birth of the twins). He advised her of the importance of the tabloid press, popular radio programmes and women's magazines. And so it was that she underwent a makeover at the hands of *Woman's Own*. The magazine's editor, Jane Reed, describes how Mrs Thatcher gave a whole afternoon to the exercise, which took place in her house, where she made tea for everyone in 'her impeccably tidy kitchen'. At one stage she had to be photographed in a wonderful, long evening dress – so long, in fact, that she had to stand on a pile of telephone directories in order for the shot to be taken. She loved the whole thing and, true to type, took it all very seriously.

She realised that her voice needed improvement. She went to a voice coach from the National Theatre. As a result she managed to lower her voice, and gained approval for the result at a meeting with Sir Laurence Olivier.

Her hair was all-important to her, as it is to many women. She was much persuaded of the utility of heated rollers and took them on overseas trips with her, frequently offering to lend them to staff who were accompanying her. The hairdresser came to No. 10 at least three times a week, so that her hair would always look its best. She was very interested in fashion and would check what was being worn in Paris before visiting France. She strongly believed that to look immaculate at all times was an integral part of the job, and that it indicated that you were an organised and controlled person, important if you were a woman in an overwhelmingly male world. She also, quite clearly, enjoyed clothes, make-up and dressing well. It may even have been a relaxation for her, a kind of feminine hinterland into which she could allow herself to retreat, on the grounds that it was all part of the job.

She took advice from her great friend Mrs Cynthia Crawford, who organised her wardrobe so that the Prime Minister could change outfits quickly. Special occasions, like state visits or royal banquets, required outstanding but not overwhelming outfits, like the wonderful gown, designed and made by Aquascutum, which she once wore for the annual Lord Mayor's Banquet in the Guildhall, a great City and government occasion. It was a fabulous gold and black fur-trimmed evening suit, against which her blonde coiffure looked dazzling under the Guildhall lights.

Her clothes aroused great interest, which endures in some circles to this day. *The Times* of 31 August 2012 announced a sale of some of Mrs Thatcher's clothes with the headline: 'The closet that ruled the Cabinet: your chance to be an Iron Lady'. Nicolas Martineau of Christie's, who were organising the sale, said, 'She was the ultimate power dresser. She was very aware of the power of television and the power it could have, and she dressed accordingly.'

Before the 1987 election she decided that she needed, again, to update her appearance. Her adviser, Margaret King of Aquascutum, told Brenda Maddox that 'She was a delight to dress. She loved trying on clothes and would twirl around like a little girl. She loved materials and buttons and told me about her mother, Beatrice, who was a dressmaker.' In the end she was the complete master of power dressing, and although she was mocked and lampooned for it, she set a style for a generation.

She also appeared on a BBC programme in November 1986, *The Englishwoman's Wardrobe*. She was asked to discuss her clothes, and the viewer was treated to a sartorial history lesson during the course of the programme as she said things like, 'This is very special, a silk dress, we take great care of this, it has to be dry-cleaned, I wore it all the way through the Falklands.' She also confided that her underclothes came from Marks and Spencer.

I have a particular memory of this because some years later, I was asked if I would take part in a similar programme, but for radio. With deep misgivings I did so, although what possible interest my wardrobe of M&S and wellington boots could have aroused, history does not reveal.

Lady Warnock, a prominent academic responsible, among many other achievements during her distinguished career, for the Warnock Report, watched the Prime

Minister on the BBC television programme, and found it 'quite obscene. The clothes showed a woman packaged together in a way that's not exactly vulgar, just "low"...' (Young, *One of Us*). This comment is uncharacteristically harsh from Lady Warnock. But many other women were fascinated to watch Margaret Thatcher discussing such feminine matters. Lady Warnock's sharp criticism does illustrate one truth, however, and that is that a woman Prime Minister is criticised not just for her policies and demeanour, but also, simply, for being a woman.

More than twenty years after she left office, there are indications that, at last, commentators, including feminists, are beginning to understand that fundamental fact.

Take the comments of India Knight, a columnist for the *Sunday Times*, writing on 20 November 2011, ahead of the release in January 2012 of the film *The Iron Lady*.

Here is a horrible and profoundly discombobulating thought: what if Margaret Thatcher was really quite – cough, choke – impressive all along? What if she wasn't in fact the one woman it was OK for feminists to hate (a problematic concept in itself)? What if she and her terrifyingly freakazoid, outsize balls of steel, to go with her terrifyingly outsized, freakazoid politics, were more worthy of our admiration than of our disgust and contempt? Believe me, this thought makes me feel iller than it makes you feel. But it is perhaps a thought worth entertaining...

Much of my generation hated her; some of us still

believe that everything that is broken about Britain today is the direct consequence of something that she personally took the hammer to – the underclass that she created by not only destroying jobs but also by selling off social housing, for example.

I bore you with my politics only to try to convey the violent dislike in which she is still held by many people my age, more than twenty years after she left office... ('A feminist icon (even to a leftie like me); *The Times*, 20 November 2011)

But here India Knight takes an unexpected turn. She continues,

In a world that is forever fretting about women and the work–life balance, it is unexpectedly refreshing to look up at the screen and see someone who just gets on with it, as we all have to do, whatever our jobs are. So now, on top of everything else, you find yourself sympathising with Thatcher over the question of children and work and her regrets at not having spent enough time with the former – regrets that, to be honest, we will all have when we're eighty. Just like Maggie.

In *The Iron Lady*, the parallels between today and the 1980s are deliberate and striking: high unemployment, London roaring with demonstrations and street protests, the urgent need for economic reform. You can almost hear cinema audiences, come January and the film's general release, muttering, 'At least she had a plan; at least she got things done.'

She points out that in the film *The Iron Lady*,

> History has been rewritten to make it look as if there were no other female MPs when Thatcher first took her seat, allowing for a marvellous shot of a blue dress and hat in a sea of grey suits, like a hydrangea surrounded by dull old bits of rock.
>
> It hasn't, however, been rewritten when it comes to the snobbery and prejudice that she encounters all along the way, from an early meeting with a braying, old-school Tory selection committee, all strangulated vowels and sniffy disdain, to her later dealings with the equally strangulated brayings and prejudices of her own Cabinet.

Could it be that at last feminist opinion is realising the scale of Margaret Thatcher's achievement, merely in becoming Britain's first woman Prime Minister? Can feminists, and other critics for that matter, begin to separate perfectly legitimate criticism of her policies from their personal criticism of her as a woman? And can feminist opinion makers at last accept that, unlike them, she did not simply rail against an unfair world, but against the odds, beat it, got there, did it?

I am given hope by an article by Caitlin Moran, one of today's most prominent young feminist writers. In it, she describes the difficulty faced by all women in the public eye. Her comments also apply to much of the hostile comment endured by Margaret Thatcher throughout her career.

Currently, every time a woman in the public eye does something, she doesn't do it just for, and as, herself. She does it on behalf of 3.3 billion other women, too. She is seen to represent her entire gender ... in a way men just aren't. ('No more opinions about women', *The Times* magazine, 15 September 2012)

Moran pleads that women should be judged for what they do as individuals, and not as representatives of their gender, because, as she writes in her incomparable style, 'we don't have time for another 100,000 years of women being held back by pinheads'.

Jill Knight puts the same thought another way.

Looking back, it seems surprising that Parliament took almost 100 years to go from having no women at all, to having the 143 we have today, in 2012, even though the few women who did make it through-out those years proved their competence – they were not just good, they did excellent work as chairmen, Whips, Privy Councillors, Peers, Speakers, Secretaries of State, and even as Prime Minister.

Virginia Bottomley sums up Margaret Thatcher's achievement:

I shall always feel privileged to have worked for a woman who so profoundly altered Britain and our place in the world. Equally she transformed opportunities for women simply through her personal example, splendidly undertaking a hugely demanding role that no female had previously secured in this country.

And that is the point. Critics ask what Margaret Thatcher did for women. The answer, in brief, is that she proved a woman could become Prime Minister of Britain, and in so doing, she pushed the barriers forward for all women, not just in this country, but throughout the world.

EPILOGUE

SIC TRANSIT GLORIA MUNDI

The end of Margaret Thatcher's career, when it came in November 1990, seemed very sudden. In fact, the storm clouds had been gathering since at least the tenth anniversary of her becoming Prime Minister, in 1989. There had been a lunch at the Savoy to mark the occasion, and I remember the whole parliamentary party streaming back along the sunny Embankment to get back to the Commons for the start of business at 2.30. Some were saying at that time that it might be wise for her to step down at the height of her popularity, and it is true that within the constituency and the country she had become a very controversial figure. Many felt that she had slain her dragons and that it would be better to have a less confrontational figure in charge of the party. There was undoubtedly plotting inside and outside Parliament, although I was too humbly placed to be aware of just how much.

There was much tut-tutting when Sir Anthony Meyer,

the gentlemanly but eccentric MP for Clwyd North West, announced in the autumn of 1989 that he would stand against her in the annual leadership election. Most of us felt this was ridiculous, but of course he was a stalking horse, and a forerunner of events to come.

Michael Heseltine was on the back benches when I arrived in the House in 1987; he had resigned eighteen months earlier over the Westland debacle. He made occasional appearances, strolling through the lobbies with his blond mane visible above the general scrum. There were those said to be 'in his camp', like Julian Critchley, Michael Mates and Keith Hampson, but apart from the odd rude reference to 'she who must be obeyed' from the naughty Critchley, much of what went on was well below the surface.

The challenge, when it came in the autumn of 1990, electrified the party and the country. Some colleagues, like Emma Nicholson, immediately declared for Heseltine. Edwina Currie equivocated. During the period leading up to the first vote, the Conservative women MPs had arranged a dinner to discuss policies for women. It was cancelled because loyalists like Jill Knight would not sit at the same table with Emma and Edwina.

Margaret Thatcher's team included Peter Morrison, her PPS, and John Moore who had left the Cabinet only a year earlier. On the night before the first vote, they were in the Tea Room, not their usual habitat. I asked if they needed any help in garnering support for Mrs Thatcher. 'Oh, no thanks,' they chorused in unison. 'We have everything under control.' It did not feel at all like that to me. I knew no one who had been canvassed for their support, and to this day I believe she was let down by her so-called campaign team. When the result came, it had to be broken to her while she was at an international gathering with President Mitterand at Versailles, in the full glare of worldwide media attention.

Janet Fookes had helped officiate at the fateful count. She writes,

> *I was also fated to see her downfall in a very particular way, as I was asked by the then Chairman of the 1922 Committee, Cranley Onslow, to help with counting the votes in the leadership election in November 1990, where she just missed securing the majority she needed to avoid a second vote. I had been surprised and a little nervous at being invited to take part in the procedure and when I had to retrieve a few ballot papers that had fallen to the floor, I felt more keenly than ever the awesome responsibility in ensuring that the count was conducted impeccably, ending as it did the remarkable career of our first British woman Prime Minister.*

The next day, 21 November 1989, we as junior ministers were consulted by our boss, Tony Newton, on whether we thought Margaret Thatcher should stand down or, as she had put it, fight on. My own view was that she had been irremediably damaged by the vote and the loss of authority that resulted from it. All members of the government were consulted in that way, and the results fed back to her in individual meetings during the evening with Cabinet ministers at No. 10. Afterwards, she wrote in *The Downing Street Years*, 'I had lost the Cabinet's support. I could not even muster a credible campaign team. It was the end.'

Frank Field also went to No. 10 that night.

In my final meeting with Mrs T. as Prime Minister, the chemistry between us changed from my earlier audiences with her, asking her to act, to a meeting with a lady, already shrunken and looking anxiously into my eyes as she asked why I had come. 'It is to tell you that you are finished,' was my reply. 'It is so unfair,' was her retort. 'I am not discussing fairness, Prime Minister, I am discussing your options.' 'It is so unfair,' came her reply, quickly building into a refrain. 'You cannot now go out on a top note. The only option available is a high note.' 'It is so unfair,' she echoed. 'You need to plan your exit tonight. If you are still Prime Minister when you go into tomorrow's censure debate, your side will tear you apart.'

I was no longer debating with the great lady. It was more of a talk between a grandmother and a grandson. 'Who will succeed me?' 'John Major, of course,' came my reply. 'Why do you say John Major?' she asked. 'You have been preparing him, haven't you, in giving him that range of top jobs?' A puzzled look appeared on Mrs T.'s face. 'He is very young,' she said. 'Time will take care of that, Prime Minister.'

The conversation came to an end. Mrs T. told me that I would be shown out by a different way into Whitehall. I resisted. An unmanned TV camera in Downing Street had recorded my coming in. It would be an even better story if it did not record my exit. The old relationship briefly reasserted itself. 'You will be leaving by a different exit.'

She knew the media's habits. The press, who enquired of her private office about who the Prime Minister saw that evening, were given a list of attendees, excluding myself. The Prime Minister believed that any reference to me would be harmful, and, before writing up that evening for publication, I sought her permission in mentioning this last kind Prime Ministerial act.

I was in the House the next day for her valedictory speech opposing the opposition's censure motion. The beginning of her delivery was through a husky voice as, I thought, she choked back those tears that were ready to fall. Then Dave Nellist, a Labour MP, intervened. 'If the record is so good, why are they sacking you?' The Prime Minister was away. 'I am enjoying this,' she said.

Much of the House began to file out of the Chamber as soon as she sat down. I went to stand at the Bar of the House. Our eyes met. I nodded approval and her eyes filled up. I turned to leave, wondering if I would ever see a Prime Minister of this rank again.

I am still waiting.

On 17 December 1990, *The House* magazine carried an interview with Margaret Thatcher, conducted by Fiona Millar. This was just two weeks after her whole life and its purpose had crashed into ruins.

In general terms I wouldn't change any of the policies if I had my time again, and no, no, no, I don't spend my time regretting. I am just getting on with the next job in hand. There's a little poem, 'Does the road wind uphill all the way? Yes, to the very end.' That's my life. I'm still going uphill, and it has been uphill as you've seen for the last two weeks. But if you believe passionately and do something that is really worthwhile you will get opposition from people who believe differently, so my life will always be uphill all the way ... Principles remain the same; they have a message for present and future generations. To distil that message, to persuade others of its validity and relevance, that will be my continuing purpose.

But her memoirs reveal the depth of her hurt.

I was sick at heart. I could have resisted the opposition of opponents and potential rivals and even respected them for it; but what grieved me was the desertion of those I had always considered friends and allies, and the weasel words whereby they had transmuted their betrayal into frank advice and concern for my fate.

And Harvey Thomas writes the revealing last words.

After she had resigned, around March 1991, she was staying at a friend's flat in Great College Street. I visited, and we sat around an open fire and chatted. The thing I remember, as we reflected on the events of late 1990 when she stepped down and handed over to John Major, was her very sad comment, 'I suppose I should have found out which of my Cabinet friends were real friends and which were false ones, shouldn't I?'

APPENDIX

'WOMEN IN A CHANGING WORLD'

On 26 July 1982, Margaret Thatcher gave the first Dame Margery Corbett Ashby memorial lecture. It is reproduced in full here.

Madame Chairman, my Lords, Ladies and Gentlemen, as you know July is a particularly busy month for politicians and ministers but I agreed to come and give this lecture out of supreme respect for Dame Margery [Dame Margery Corbett Ashby] and because I was very honoured to be invited to be the first person to give this memorial lecture.

The life and work of Dame Margery spanned almost a century, from her birth in 1882 to her death last year. And rarely, I think, has a century so exemplified Disraeli's maxim that in a progressive country change is constant. Dame Margery, who was instrumental in bringing about so much change, was herself born into a world of change.

And I want just to develop the theme. 1882 was a world of change. She was born into a world of change. She brought about so much change and what now are we going to do in the future, to transmit the very best of the truths that have been handed down to us, to future generations?

Let's have a look at the kind of changes that were taking place in 1882 – when she was born.

It was a world of political change where not only women were deprived. It is obvious that the issue of women's right to vote arises only when people's right to vote has been established, or at least is on the agenda. And for most of human history it has been absent. In 1882 only 33 per cent of men had the right to vote. Two years later the Reform Bill doubled that percentage, extending civil rights to an extra two million men.

It was a world of educational change. Elementary education had just been made compulsory by an act of 1880. Schools and colleges for women were springing up. Newnham College, Cambridge, where Dame Margery was to take a degree in classics, had been founded in 1871.

It was a world of scientific and religious change. In 1882 Charles Darwin, whose theory of evolution had challenged many accepted beliefs and disturbed many faiths and brought about a radical change in all human thought, was buried in Westminster Abbey, to the disgust of many churchmen. Some years earlier, Bishop Samuel Wilberforce of Oxford, in his argument with the Darwinians, had shown the typically Victorian chivalrous attitude to women. He said that he could accept that his grandfather might have been descended from an ape, but not his grandmother.

It was a world of social change, much of it generated by the numerous voluntary organisations founded at that time. Their names read like a roll-call of compassion. The National Society for the Prevention of Cruelty to Children founded in 1884, the St John Ambulance Association in 1887, the Soldiers, Sailors and Airmen's Families Association in 1885, the Church Army in 1890 – and many, many more. They were years of voluntary activity. They were years of enormous confidence in the future.

It was a world in which we were just beginning to see the first glimmer of change in the professional status of women – for example, in nursing and medicine. Elizabeth Garrett Anderson had qualified in 1865. You'll recall, Madame Chairman, that the suffragettes did not fight for the right of women to work because so many women had of necessity to go out to work. Indeed Shaftesbury had commented adversely on that trend when he said: 'Domestic life and domestic discipline must soon be at an end; society will consist of individuals no longer grouped into families.'

In 1881 some 27 per cent of the female population of the United Kingdom already worked outside the home. It's interesting that today the percentage is only 32 – not so very different from or not so very many more than that time. We think that women going out to work is a new thing. We tend to forget that during those extremely difficult years of the last century, so many had to go out to work and often do work which was distasteful to them.

What Dame Margery and her generation did fight for was the right of women to be admitted to the professions – the law, the civil service and the Diplomatic Service.

It was, also that year, a world of legal change – and those of you who are lawyers will remember that it was the Married Women's Property Act that was passed in 1882. It affected a major advance in women's rights. Before that time no married woman had been allowed to hold property of her own. It automatically passed to her husband on marriage. From that time, women were then allowed to retain and own property independently of their husbands. This reasonable measure, which stopped the married woman from being a mere chattel of her husband, caused much distress in its passage through Parliament. And I did one or two very interesting bits of research.

One Member felt that its enactment should be delayed until 1885:

'In order,' he said, 'to give men who were contemplating matrimony, time to change their minds when they found the law altered.'

Another feared that:

'No man would marry a woman with property, knowing that she could set him at defiance – the Bill was against Scripture.'

He had obviously never reflected on the words of the marriage service when, as the man said:

'... with all my worldly goods I thee endow.'

Until then, for women who had property, it had really been the other way round.

So Dame Margery was born into a world of change, the educational change, the social change, the political change, the legal change, the scientific change. And really change is an essential characteristic of the human condition. But history is shaped by the way in which men and women respond to that change. They may resist it absolutely, so that all its opportunities are wasted, like the religious sect who will not use buttons because they regard them as a product of a decadent modern civilisation. Or they may accept change so wholeheartedly that novelty becomes a virtue in itself and all the lessons of history and experience are just dismissed. This attitude has caused much political upheaval, as whole regimes and civilisations have some-times been swept away in the name of change which is assumed to be beneficent just because it is change.

Then there is another response that is one which welcomes and uses change, but refuses to be ruled by it, testing each new development against the eternal verities.

I believe that this last was the attitude of Dame Margery in her great contributions to the century of change through which she lived, in her services to women and society, in Britain and throughout the world. She was co-founder of the Townswomen's Guilds, of the Commonwealth Countries League and the National Women Citizens Association. She was President of the International Women's Suffrage

Alliance from 1923 to 1946 and an office-bearer in it for seventy years. She gave her first presidential speech at the Sorbonne in 1926, soon after I was born. She presided at Berlin in 1929, Istanbul in 1935, Copenhagen in 1939 and Interlaken in 1946. What a fantastic record she had.

Her first concern was that women should have the same political rights as men. With that end in view she became Secretary of the National Union of Women's Suffrage Societies as far back as 1907 working tirelessly until full adult female suffrage was achieved in 1928. Some of you will recall that women first got the vote in 1918, but only women who were aged over thirty. I think it's the only time in legislation when the year thirty has been of legal significance in a woman's life. And then in 1928 on the same terms as men.

The task was not made easier – the task of women's suffrage when Dame Margery took it up – wasn't made easier by the fact that the leader of her chosen party, Mr Asquith, was resolutely opposed to votes for women. He followed the tradition of Mr Gladstone, who in 1884 and then Prime Minister, had spoken against women's suffrage. He – and I quote – 'feared that voting would trespass upon their delicacy, their purity, their refinement, the elevation of their whole nature'.

Dame Margery is proof that it did none of those things. It is of course true – and I should make a clean breast of it – that Winston Churchill had often felt the same way about women in political life. And when I went to see Lady

Churchill, shortly after I became Leader of the Party –
because I wanted to see her, she was a wonderful woman
in her own right – and she reminded me of this; and she
said, '…but you know I always used to argue with Winston
over it'. And I guess she did.

I am very conscious of the fact that it is due to the efforts
of Margery Corbett Ashby and others like her, that women
today are able to play such a major part in political life. All
women received the vote in 1928 and 1929 saw the appointment of the first woman Cabinet minister, Margaret
Bondfield. But this wasn't enough for Dame Margery.
In her speech of that year to the British Commonwealth
League, she deplored the fact that women did not have the
right to sit in the House of Lords. Almost thirty years later,
in 1958, the Life Peerages Act gave women that right. This
was extended in 1963 when the same government admitted hereditary peeresses to the House of Lords.

Last year we achieved another 'first' when I asked
Baroness Young, who has done so much for public life, to
become the first woman leader of the Upper House. I like
to think that Dame Margery would have approved.

In the House of Commons, more than half a century
after all women got the vote, there are only twenty-one
women Members of Parliament out of a House of 635
Members. And I think this would have been a great disappointment to the early suffragettes whose main fight was
for the rights of women to full participation in politics,
local government and the community. They did this partly

because it is just and equitable that women should have such rights; but also because they wanted public life to be shaped and influenced by the special talents and experiences of women.

To quote Dame Margery again, in her 1926 Presidential Address to the Congress of the International Alliance at Paris:

> No woman is so busy in her home or profession that she can't by a better adjustment of her time, spare some energy to work for neighbours, her town and her country. We seek to deepen a woman's sense of responsibility and to widen her sphere of activity from the home to the city, from the city to the nation.

My generation put it in virtually the same way, when we say that the home should be the centre but not the boundary of a woman's life.

Now what are these special talents and experiences which women have to bring to public life? Are they any different in kind from those of men? Yes – I think they are, because we women bear the children and create and run the home. It is noticeable, Madame Chairman, that many of the suffragettes were very womanly. Like Dame Margery, they had the inestimable privilege of being wives and mothers and they pursued their public work against the background of full and happy domestic lives. They neglected no detail of those lives – so that they were warm as well as immensely capable women. And it was these enriched lives, with their breadth of experience, that they devoted to public service.

The many practical skills and management qualities needed to make a home – and I often stress to audiences that you have to be a manager to run a home – those many management qualities give women an ability to deal with a variety of problems and to do so quickly. And it's that versatility and decisiveness which is so valuable in public life. And I may say that I think I am able to make decisions at a tremendous speed in public life because I have been used to doing that in the home. It also means that one is able, quite naturally, to deal with an enormous volume of work and to switch your mind to whatever problem is at hand. Indeed I sometimes think it wouldn't be a bad maxim in life if you said, 'what we have to do, and do well, is the very next job that comes to hand'.

Now, after the victory for women's suffrage had been won here Dame Margery went on to work for it in other countries, through the International Alliance. Their 1935 Congress was held in Turkey where, despite promises and statements of relevant legislative intent in 1930, 1931 and 1934, Turkish women had still not received the vote. So, on her arrival in Istanbul, Dame Margery told the Mayor that it was a pity 'that women will come from all over the world to Turkey and find Turkish women without the vote'.

That remark found its way to the President of Turkey – President Ataturk – and very soon Turkish women had been granted the vote on the same terms as men and seventeen women Members of Parliament were elected. What quiet power Dame Margery had.

It was also after 1928 that she turned to the second great strand of her work, your Guilds, the Townswomen's Guilds, born in 1929 out of the earlier suffrage societies. The significant achievements of the Townswomen's Guilds in the last half-century owe much to her example and her vigour. And it is useful to remind ourselves of the objectives which guide your work:

> To advance the education of women, irrespective of race, creed or party, so as to enable them to make the best contribution towards the common good: To educate women in the principles of good citizenship and to provide facilities for women to improve their own social conditions and those of their fellows.

I understand you've modified that latter part a little now. It reads in a much more modern way; but you know, so many things, they're not always quite so clear as the older ones. So I thought I would take the older one. You know, it still expresses really what we stand for and what we set out to do.

Now, of course, Dame Margery worked hard for legislative change. She and others knew that only legislation could give women the vote and certain fundamental rights. But she knew too that legislation is not enough. As she said when I was privileged to share a platform with her in Westminster Hall in 1978, at the celebration of fifty years of women's suffrage: 'It's comparatively easy to change the law. What is difficult is to change the attitudes of the community.'

She set out to change those attitudes through the Townswomen's Guilds, and her work in them illustrated the belief that legislation can provide only a foundation for action. And the rest is up to us. To give a person a vote is a remarkable achievement, but to help people to understand how democracy works, and its dependence on the exercise of personal responsibility, is much harder. And is that not part of the role of the Townswomen's Guilds?

The benefits which law is intended to promote can only be actually achieved by the effort of individuals. A government may provide incentives for industrial development, but it is the brains and hands of men and women which must translate that into action and industrial health – and success.

A government may provide a framework of social services, a safety net through which none may fall. But the many deeds of mercy, the myriad acts of human kindness which give life its dignity and meaning, these are the work of individuals. And no state can ever play the part of a good neighbour. The loving care which should generate and inform such activities is a feature not of legislation but of the human spirit. It cannot be manufactured or decreed by politicians.

'What's the government going to do about it?' is a

common phrase. I hear it often! I shall hear it when I get back to Number 10 tonight! But surely the better approach was that expressed by President Kennedy in his Innaugural Address: 'Ask not what your country can do for you. Ask what you can do for your country.'

Recently, Madame Chairman, this summer, we have seen that philosophy abundantly fulfilled by our people when called up to defend freedom and justice, many thousands of miles away.

The achievements for which we honour Dame Margery today, although great in themselves, have been a comparatively small part of the enormous changes which have transformed our lives over the years.

Changes in transport, in communications, automation, fuel and energy, science and medicine, in the environment and in our cities. Above all, changes in the standard of prosperity so that the luxuries of the few have become the necessities of the many. It is not therefore possible to isolate the effect of the changing status of women in our society. Nevertheless if we are to shape our future, we must take a dispassionate look at what has happened to the structure of society across the century.

Throughout history, great emphasis has been laid upon the importance of the family. But in family matters today there are some very disquieting features. For example, in 1882 there were 43,000 illegitimate births in England and Wales. Some eighty years later, in 1960, there were approximately the same number and proportion. In 1980 the numbers had risen from 43,000 to 77,000. Worse still, the number of girls who conceived children under the age of sixteen, had risen from 6,600 in 1970 to 8,100 in 1979. Further, the number of juvenile offenders has doubled in less than twenty years, rising from 100,000 in 1965 to nearly 200,000 in 1979. Moreover, today, one in ten marriages is expected to break down after five years and one in three after thirty years.

It is, of course, difficult to make valid comparisons with a century ago. But the figures do tell us what has happened in the last twenty years and we can't fail to be worried by them. Indeed, I wonder whether the family has been sufficiently highly regarded in recent years. Much emphasis has been placed on individual rights, less on our duties to each other.

Children have been encouraged to grow up faster and to see themselves as independent of parents. Parents have been told by self-appointed experts that their duties to each other and to their children should be balanced by more emphasis on self fulfilment. In other words, we have seen the birth of the permissive society. Has that benefited women? Far from it.

Women know that society is founded on dignity, reticence and discipline. We know instinctively that the disintegration of society begins with the death of idealism and convention.

We know that our society as a whole, and especially for the children, much depends upon the family unit remaining secure and respected. It is significant that so many women who have reached the top have families of their own, like Dame Margery and, as I can personally testify, they are our greatest joy and our strength.

It is of course true that women of our generation are often still comparatively young by the time our children are grown up and therefore we have an opportunity further to develop our own talents, an opportunity which in Dame Margery's day, was rarely available. For many, that experience can enhance their lives and enlarge their interests. But I remain totally convinced that when children are young, however busy we may be with practical duties inside or outside the home, the most important thing of all is to devote enough time and care to the children's needs and problems. There are some things for which only a parent will do. I'll never forget the comment of a headmaster of a school I visited when I was Secretary of State for Education. He said to me that as many problem children came from rich as poor homes. Some were from homes where the children had everything they could wish for except, perhaps, enough of their parents' attention. Madame President, material goods can never be a substitute for loving care. Too much money can create problems as well as solve them.

The battle for women's rights has been largely won. The days when they were demanded and discussed in strident tones should be gone forever. And I hope they are. I hated those strident tones that you still hear from some Women's Libbers.

The battle is largely won, but we must now see women's rights in perspective and turn our attention to how we could use human rights to build the kind of world we wish our children to grow up in.

It's no use looking through rose-tinted spectacles or pretending that human imperfections and evil will disappear if we get the economy right. They won't. They are as old as humanity itself and we have to fight them constantly. Fight them by making and enforcing laws to protect the weak; by upholding conventions and customs which serve the larger purpose and which limit the selfish purpose.

In international affairs the only protection for civilised values against the tyrant is a sure defence. Dame Margery's generation learned that so vividly and at so great a price. It is a tragedy that since the last World War there have been, I'm going to tell you how many conflicts since the last World War. You will be amazed when I say the number, as I was amazed when I did the research. Since the last World War, there have been over one hundred and forty conflicts in various parts of the world and they continue even as we meet here today.

The danger for democracy is that too many people will say, what can one person do among 55 million? Dame Margery never took that view. Nor does your society of Guilds. Politicians will know that Burke put it so well, so long ago: 'All that is necessary for evil to triumph is for good men (and women) to do nothing.'

But our generation has reason to be thankful that those noble and brave acts which brought fame and renown to

Britain's name are matched by deeds of courage and valour in our time. And we saw that over the Falklands story.

Madame Chairman, it's a rare honour to be Prime Minister of the United Kingdom. It is a supreme privilege to occupy that high office when great human causes have to be defended. It has been an inspiration to witness the young generation of today set the most glorious standards for the young of tomorrow.

I'm very much aware of how much I owe to Dame Margery. I honour and thank her for her sense of purpose, for her selfless service and for that tireless spirit which sustained her until her works were well and truly accomplished.

That was where I had finished writing this Lecture and as I looked up, on my desk, at Chequers, I opened the top of the ink stand. There is there, a saying in Latin, which fortunately is translated into English, which I thought was so appropriate, both for Dame Margery and for those principles by which I try to guide my stewardship, and I finish with it:

To stand on the ancient ways
To see which is the right and good way,
And in that way to walk.

CONTRIBUTORS

Some of the writers have themselves provided the career details they wish to be included. For the others, I have given relevant details drawn from *Who's Who* and *Dod's Parliamentary Companion*.

ALSTON John, CBE, DL
Leader, Norfolk County Council 1981–1987 and 1989–1993. Chairman, Norfolk Health Authority 1996–2002. Chairman, Norfolk Strategic Partnership 2002–2007. High Sheriff of Norfolk 2004–2005.

ARMSTRONG Robert, The Lord Armstrong of Ilminster, GCB, CVO
Secretary of the Cabinet 1979–1987.

BEESLEY Ian, FRSA
Official Historian, Cabinet Office 2007–present. Deputy Head of Efficiency Unit 1981–1983. Under-Secretary and Official Head of Unit 1983–1986.

BOOTH Hartley, OBE
Chairman of Uzbek–British Trade and Industry Council since

1999. Special Adviser at 10 Downing Street 1984–1988. CEO British Urban Development 1988–1990. MP for Finchley 1992–1997.

BOTTOMLEY Virginia, The Rt. Hon. the Baroness Bottomley of Nettlestone, DL
MP for Surrey South West 1984–2005. Secretary of State for Health 1992–1995. Secretary of State for National Heritage 1995–1997.

BRUNSON Michael, OBE
Writer and broadcaster. Political Editor of ITN 1986–2000. ITN Washington Correspondent 1972–1977.

BYFORD Hazel, The Baroness Byford of Rothley, DBE, DL
Conservative activist and member of Conservative Women's National Committee. Chairman of same 1990–1993. President of Conservative National Union 1996–1997. Opposition spokesman, House of Lords, on Environment, Agriculture and Rural Affairs 1998–2007.

CHALKER Lynda, The Rt. Hon. the Baroness Chalker of Wallasey
MP for Wallasey 1974–1992. Opposition spokesman, DHSS 1976–1979. Parliamentary Under-Secretary, DHSS 1979–1982, Department of Transport 1982–1983. Minister of State, Department of Transport 1983–1986, Foreign and Commonwealth Office 1986–1997. Minister for Overseas Development, 1989–1992.

CORMACK Patrick, The Lord Cormack of Enville, DL, FSA
Patrick Cormack was a South Staffordshire Member of Parliament from 1970 until 2010. He was a member of the team which, under the late Airey Neave, worked for the election of Margaret Thatcher as Leader of the Conservative Party in 1975. In 1978, he edited *Right Turn*, a collection of essays by former Labour supporters, including the late Reg Prentice, who

had decided to back the Thatcher Conservative Party in the 1979 election.

COTTRELL Elizabeth

Director of Research, Centre for Policy Studies 1980–1984. Special Adviser to Richard Luce, Minister for the Arts and the Civil Service 1987–1990. Special Adviser to Gillian Shephard at Departments of Employment, Agriculture, Education, and Education and Employment 1992–1997.

FIELD Frank, The Rt. Hon.

MP for Birkenhead 1979 to present. Director, Child Poverty Action Group 1969–1979, Low Pay Unit, 1974–1978. Chairman of DSS Select Committee 1987–1990. Minister of State DSS 1997–1998.

FOOKES Janet, The Baroness Fookes of Plymouth, DBE

MP for Merton and Morden 1970–1974. MP for Plymouth Drake 1974–1997. A Deputy Speaker of the House of Commons 1992–1997. A Deputy Speaker in the House of Lords, 2002 to the present.

GARNER, Sir Anthony

Director of Organisation at Conservative Central Office 1976–1988, following a distinguished career in the Grenadier Guards and in the Conservative Party organisation.

HOWE Geoffrey, The Rt. Hon. the Lord Howe of Aberavon, CH, QC

MP for Bebington 1964–1966. MP for Reigate 1970–1974. MP for Surrey East 1974–1992. Chancellor of the Exchequer 1979–1983. Foreign Secretary 1983–1989. Lord President of the Council, Leader of the House of Commons and Deputy Prime Minister 1989–1990.

HURD Douglas, The Rt. Hon. the Lord Hurd of Westwell, CH, CBE

MP for Mid Oxfordshire 1974–1983. MP for Witney 1983–1997.

Secretary of State for Northern Ireland 1984–1985. Home Secretary 1985–1989. Foreign Secretary 1989–1995.

JOINER Sarah
PA for the Leader's Tours, Conservative Central Office, February to August 1979.

JOPLING Michael, The Rt. Hon. the Lord Jopling of Ainderby Quernhow, DL
MP for Westmorland 1964–1983. MP for Westmorland and Lonsdale 1983–1997. Government Chief Whip 1979–1983. Minister of Agriculture, Fisheries and Food 1983–1987.

KING Tom, The Rt. Hon. the Lord King of Bridgwater, CH
MP for Bridgwater 1970–2001. Cabinet member under Margaret Thatcher 1983–1992 at Environment, Transport, Employment, Northern Ireland and Defence.

KNIGHT Jill, The Baroness Knight of Collingtree, DBE
MP for Edgbaston 1966–1997. Vice-Chairman, 1922 Committee 1988–1997. Member, Council of Europe 1977–1988, Chair 1999–2010. Fellow, Industry and Parliament Trust.

LOUSSOUARN Sophie
Lecturer at the Sorbonne and at the University of Amiens, visiting professor at the University of Alicante. Commentator on British politics and economy on French radio and television.

LUCAS Jean, MBE
Organiser for the Young Conservatives and for forty-five years a Conservative Party agent, retiring in 2002. Chairman of the Conservative Agents 1980.

MACGREGOR John, The Rt. Hon. the Lord MacGregor of Pulham Market, OBE
MP for South Norfolk 1974–2001. Chief Secretary to the Treasury 1985–1987. Minister of Agriculture, Fisheries and Food 1987–1989. Secretary of State, Education and Science 1989–1990. Lord

President of the Council and Leader of the House of Commons 1990–1992. Secretary of State for Transport 1992–1994. Chairman of the Association of Conservative Peers 2010 to present.

MAJOR John, The Rt. Hon. Sir John Major, KG, CH
MP for Huntingdonshire 1979–1983. MP for Huntingdon 1983–2001. Foreign Secretary 1989. Chancellor of the Exchequer 1989–1990. Prime Minister and First Lord of the Treasury 1990–1997.

MILLER Doreen, The Baroness Miller of Hendon, MBE
Conservative activist since 1970. Candidate in 1984 Euro election and in 1986 ILEA election. Served for many years on Conservative Women's National Committee. Frontbench spokesman in House of Lords on Trade and Industry 1993–2007.

MONKS John, The Lord John Monks
General Secretary of the TUC, 1993–2003.

PARSONS Richard, Sir Richard Parsons, KCMG
A member of the British Foreign Service 1951–1988. Posts held include Assistant Private Secretary to the Foreign Secretary, service in Washington, Laos, Argentina, Turkey and Nigeria. Ambassador to Hungary, Spain and Sweden.

PLUMB Henry, The Lord Plumb of Coleshill, DL
Prominent agriculturalist and NFU activist. MEP for Cotswolds 1979–1999. Chair, Agriculture Committee 1979–1982. Chair, European Democratic Group 1982–1987. President of the European Parliament 1987–1999.

RICHARDS Janice
Worked in Prime Minister's office 1971–1999. Head of Garden Rooms and No. 10 Correspondence Section from 1985.

RIDDELL Peter, The Rt. Hon. Peter Riddell
Director of the Institute for Government. During the Thatcher years, he was Political Editor of the *Financial Times* (1981–1988),

having been that paper's economics correspondent beforehand and its US editor afterwards. From 1991 until 2012, he was chief political commentator of *The Times*.

SECCOMBE Joan, The Baroness Seccombe, DBE
Chairman of the Conservative Women's National Committee 1981–1984. Chairman of the Party Conference 1987. Party Vice-Chairman for Women 1987–1997.

SIMPSON David, CBE
His 42-year career with the Conservative Party includes Deputy Central Office Agent, Greater London 1980–1989, and South East Regional Director 1989–1998. Head of European Organisation in CCO 1998–2001 and Head of Compliance 2001–2010.

SIMPSON Keith
MP for Mid Norfolk 1997–2010. MP for Broadland 2010 to present. Shadow Minister for Defence 2002–2005 and for Foreign Affairs 2005–2010. PPS to The Rt. Hon. William Hague, Foreign Affairs 2010 to present.

TAYLOR John, The Lord Taylor of Holbeach, CBE
Member, Executive Committee, East Midlands Area Conservative Council 1966–1998. Member, Conservative Board of Finance 1985–1989. President and Chairman of Conservative Party Conference 1997–1998. Parliamentary Under-Secretary, Home Office 2012.

THOMAS Harvey, CBE, FRSA, FCIPR, FCIJ
A PR consultant from 1976. PR consultant to the Conservative Party from 1979. Director of Press/Communication/Presentation at Conservative Central Office 1984–1991.

VÉDRINE Hubert
Diplomatic adviser to François Mitterand 1981–1988. Chief of Staff at the Élysée Palace 1991–1995. Minister for Foreign Affairs in the Jospin government 1997–2002.

WAKEHAM John, The Rt. Hon. the Lord Wakeham, DL
MP for Maldon 1974–1983. MP for South Colchester and
Maldon 1983–1992. Government Chief Whip 1983–1987. Lord
Privy Seal and Leader of the House of Commons 1987–1988.
Lord President of the Council and Leader of the House of
Commons 1988–1989. Secretary of State for Energy 1989–1992.
Lord Privy Seal and Leader of the House of Lords 1992–1994.

BIBLIOGRAPHY

Attali, Jacques, *Verbatim* (Robert Laffont, 1993)

Brunson, Michael, *A Ringside Seat* (Coronet Books, 2000)

Byron, Alan, *The Iron Lady* (A2B Media Ltd Production, 2012)

Campbell, John, *Margaret Thatcher* (Jonathan Cape, 2000)

Cradock, Percy, *In Pursuit of British Interests: Reflections on Foreign Policy under Margaret Thatcher and John Major* (John Murray, 2000)

Edwards, Giles, (ed.) *Cabinet Government* (Politico's, 2004)

Gouiffres, Pierre-François, *Margaret Thatcher face aux Mineurs* (Editions Privat, 2007)

Hansard House of Commons Official Reports

Hansard Society, *Women at the Top* (1990)

Harris, Kenneth, *Thatcher* (Weidenfeld and Nicolson, 1988)

Hennessy, Peter, *Whitehall* (Martin Secker and Warburg, 1989)

Hennessy, Peter, *The Prime Minister* (Allen Lane, 2000)

Hoskyns, John, *Just in Time: Inside the Thatcher Revolution* (Aurum Press, 2000)

Howe, Geoffrey, *Conflict of Loyalty* (Macmillan, 1994)

Jenkins, Simon, *Thatcher and Sons* (Allen Lane, 2006)

Kenny, Anthony, *A Life in Oxford* (John Murray Publishers, 1997)

King, Anthony, *Margaret Thatcher: The Style of a Prime Minister* (Duke University Press, 1985)

Knight, India, 'A feminist icon (even to a leftie like me)', *The Times*, 20 November 2011

Lucas, Jean, *Between the Thin Blue Lines* (Trafford Publishing, 2008)

McDougall, Linda, *Westminster Women* (Vintage, 1998)

Maddox, Brenda, *Maggie: The First Lady* (Hodder and Stoughton, 2003)

Major, John, *The Autobiography* (HarperCollins, 1999)

Moran, Caitlin, 'No more opinions about women', *The Times* magazine, 15 September 2012

Parris, Matthew, 'A time, a place. Two entirely different stories', *The Times*, 26 May 2012

Seldon, Anthony, *Major: A Political Life* (Weidenfeld and Nicolson, 1997)

Shephard, Gillian, *Shephard's Watch* (Politico's, 2000)

Thatcher, Margaret, *The Downing Street Years* (HarperCollins, 1993)

Thatcher, Margaret, *The Path to Power* (HarperCollins, 1995)

Young, Hugo, *One of Us* (Macmillan, 1989)

INDEX

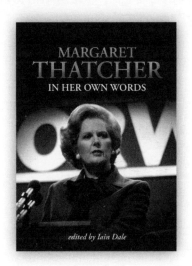

Also available from Biteback

THE MARGARET THATCHER
BOOK OF QUOTATIONS
EDITED BY IAIN DALE
AND GRANT TUCKER

Margaret Thatcher is the most quoted British political
leader since Winston Churchill and in this unique
collection Iain Dale and Grant Tucker have picked out
her most memorable remarks. Never far from emitting
a scathing rebuke she possesses a facility for the spoken
word rivalled by few others. Some quotes are funny, many
are inspirational, most are thoughtful – but they are
all unforgettable.

352pp paperback, £12.99
Available from all good bookshops or order from
www.bitebackpublishing.com